TUDOR
WOMEN

ALISON PLOWDEN

TUDOR
WOMEN
Queens and Commoners

ATHENEUM
New York
1979

Library of Congress Cataloging in Publication Data

Plowden, Alison.
    Tudor women.

        Bibliography: p.
        1. England – Social life and customs – 16th century.
    2. Tudor, House of.   3. Great Britain – History – Tudors,
    1485–1603.   4. Women – England – History.   I. Title.
    DA320.P57   1979   942.05   78–21958
    ISBN   0–689–10944–X

Manufactured in Great Britain by
Butler & Tanner Ltd, Frome and London
First American Edition

Contents

v

Illustrations

Women in
the World

The English, so most sixteenth-century Europeans agreed, were a lazy, arrogant, light-minded race. Their land was so fertile, the climate so temperate, the great tracts of forest so teemed with game, the lush pastures supported so many fat sheep and cattle that their living seemed almost indecently easy to visiting Germans and Italians, who were inclined to pass disparaging remarks about the gluttony, idleness and general unreliability of the islanders. Not that this bothered the islanders in the slightest, since their most outstanding national characteristic was a deeply ingrained contempt and suspicion of all things foreign, coupled with an unshakable conviction 'that there are no other men than themselves and no other world but England'. When entertaining a favoured foreign guest at one of their heavily-laden dinner-tables, they would ply him with food and drink, enquiring with genial condescension whether such-and-such a delicacy was to be found in *his* country; and the greatest compliment which could be paid to any handsome foreigner was to assure him that he looked like an Englishman.

The splendid self-confidence of the English was shared by their wives, and foreign tourists were all greatly struck by the amount of freedom generally enjoyed by married women. For although, as a Dutch resident in London observed, the women were entirely in the power of their husbands, they were not shut up or kept so strictly as in Spain and some other countries. On the contrary, they had free management of their households and could go out to market to buy what they liked best to eat. 'They are well-dressed,' wrote Emanuel van Meteren, 'fond of taking it easy, and commonly leave the care of household matters and drudgery to their servants. They sit before their doors, decked out in fine clothes, in order to see and be seen by the passers-by.' At feasts and banquets the ladies were shown the greatest honour, being placed at the upper end of the table and served first. The rest of their time was employed 'in walking and riding, in playing at cards or otherwise, in visiting their friends and keeping company, conversing with their equals (whom they term gossips) and their neighbours, and making merry with them at child-births, christenings, churchings and funerals; and all this with the permission and knowledge of their husbands, as such is the custom'. Their husbands, it seemed, would from time to time wistfully recommend the superior industry and care of German or Dutch housewives, but with little result. The English ladies, quite unimpressed, preferred to retain their own customs.

A German, writing in the 1590s, also commented on the fact that the womenfolk of England had far more liberty than was usual in other lands and knew just how to make good use of it; 'for they often stroll out or drive by coach in very gorgeous clothes, and the men must put up with such ways'. Earlier in the century it had been noted that even ladies of distinction could be seen drinking wine in public taverns, and their free and easy manners extended to their own homes. A Greek tourist, one Nicander Nucius, was astonished at 'the great simplicity and absence of jealousy' shown in the attitude of Englishmen towards their wives and was shocked to discover that any chance male guest was expected, indeed encouraged, to salute his hostess by kissing her on the mouth – a lack of discrimination which Nucius considered barbarous. Desiderius Erasmus, on the other hand, thought it delightful and urged an Italian poet friend of his to waste no time in coming over to England, where he would not only find 'girls with angels' faces', so kind and obliging that he would much prefer them to his Muses, but also a native custom 'never to be sufficiently recommended'. 'Wherever you come,' wrote the Sage of Rotterdam enthusiastically, 'you are received with a kiss by all; when you take your leave, you are dismissed with kisses; you return, kisses are repeated. They come to visit you, kisses again; they leave you, you kiss them all round.' Even the stiff, shy Philip of Spain, when he arrived to marry Mary Tudor, painstakingly embraced all the Queen's ladies, 'so as not to break the custom of the country, which is a good one'.

Most people agreed that English ladies were well worth kissing. It was an age which admired blue-eyed blondes, still the predominant English type, and the German Samuel Kiechel described the women of England as 'charming and by nature so mighty pretty as I have scarcely ever beheld'. An Italian captain, Francesco Ferretti, thought them 'of marvellous beauty and wonderfully clever'; while Etienne Perlin, a Frenchman who in general had very little time for England or the English, conceded Englishwomen to be 'the greatest beauties in the world, and as fair as alabaster'. They were also 'cheerful, courteous and of a good address'. A rather less complimentary note was struck by an anonymous Spaniard, who came to England in King Philip's retinue in 1554. In a letter home he remarked on the immodesty of the English ladies' short skirts and gave it as his opinion that they were neither beautiful nor graceful when dancing. 'Not a single Spanish gentleman has fallen in love with one of them nor takes any interest in them,' he wrote sourly. Here he was wrong, for one Spanish gentleman, the diplomat Count de Feria, did fall in love with an English girl and later married her. It's true that this was an exceptional case – probably the tense atmosphere between the two nations at the time was not conducive to romance – and the same correspondent maintains that Englishwomen 'are not the sort of women for whom Spaniards feel inclined to take much trouble'. But even he was moved to pay tribute to their horsemanship: 'for who, in any other land, ever saw women riding forth alone as they do here, where many of them manage their horses with consummate skill and are as firm in the saddle as any man'.

It must, of course, be remembered that the elegant and emancipated ladies who made such an impression on foreign visitors were townswomen and mostly from the prosperous and forward-looking trading and professional classes – the wives of lawyers and government officials, well-to-do merchants and City men. More typical, because far more numerous, were the countrywomen whose daily routine was governed by the inexorable demands of the land by which they lived. The farmer's wife, even the wife of the average lord of the manor, had small leisure for gossiping and card-playing, and few opportunities for jaunts.

But although the countrywoman might be less sophisticated, less fashionably dressed and carry a heavier work-load than her London counterpart, she was seldom a mere drudge. The farmer in particular depended largely on his wife's partnership for, as one writer on the subject succinctly observed: 'husbandrie weepeth, where huswiferie sleepeth'. On the vast majority of farms and smallholdings, the dairy, poultry yard and vegetable plot were regarded as the housewife's responsibility. She took her own produce to market and expected a say in the disposal of the profits. Some women became farmers on their own account, and it was not unusual for a widow to take over her late husband's farm or business and run it very efficiently.

Higher up the social scale, where husbands were often away from home for long periods, either on their own affairs or the king's service, wives would be left in sole charge of considerable estates. Almost the only surviving letter of sad, neglected Amye Robsart, wife of Queen Elizabeth's favourite man Robert Dudley, deals with a business matter, and in it Amye instructs the steward of the couple's Norfolk property 'of her own authority' to proceed with the sale of some wool to settle an outstanding debt.

Again and again foreigners, commenting on the amazing freedom and independence of Englishwomen, refer to the common saying that England was the paradise of married women, but sixteenth-century England was still very much a man's world, and for women the entry to even a limited degree of paradise depended on first acquiring a husband. Marriage might provide protection and financial security, and confer status in an intensely status-conscious society, but it also brought with it a tyranny, sometimes a martyrdom, which few wives escaped. From her mid-teens to her early forties (if she lived that long), the average woman could expect to face the ordeal of childbirth if not annually, at least upwards of a dozen times. Most women bore between eight and fifteen children and saw perhaps half of them die.

Henry VII's Queen, Elizabeth of York, reared four babies out of eight and herself died in childbirth on or about her thirty-eighth birthday. Out of nine pregnancies, Catherine of Aragon produced one surviving daughter. Anne Boleyn miscarried of the boy who might have saved her, and Jane Seymour died in her twenties from the results of bearing the longed-for male heir. The misfortunes of royalty naturally attracted the most attention, but it was a story repeated in countless other families whose domestic tragedies are recorded in brass and stone in parish churches up and down the land.

The women did not complain as they faced a constant prospect of pain, heartbreak and death. Such physical servitude had been their lot from time out of mind, and they accepted it with faithful courage while, at the same time, busily attending to the laborious round of household chores, eagerly following the latest fashion, riding abroad with a seat as firm in the saddle as any man, and showing a cheerful, courteous face to the world. These were the women of Tudor England.

CHAPTER ONE

My Lady
the King's Mother

The royal House of Tudor was to owe a great deal to its women-folk. Indeed, it owed its very existence to a woman, although when, in 1452, Henry VI was moved to bestow the wardship and marriage of Margaret, the nine-year-old Beaufort heiress, on his half-brothers Edmund and Jasper Tudor, he can have had no notion that he was assisting at the birth of a new dynasty. Henry, a monarch not normally noted for his worldly wisdom, may have been acting out of simple benevolence. He seems to have felt a strong sense of family obligation towards his young relatives, offspring of his widowed mother's enterprising second marriage to her Welsh Clerk of the Wardrobe, and had already made himself responsible for their education. His more hard-headed advisers, on the other hand, were probably considering how the support of the Tudor brothers, a promising pair of war-riors, could best be secured for the Lancastrian cause at a time when the House of Lancaster was clearly going to need all the support it could get in the approaching struggle with its Yorkist rivals. Edmund and Jasper had been created Earls of Rich-mond and Pembroke respectively but the custody of Margaret Beaufort was an even greater prize. Not merely was she her father's heir, and the late John Beaufort, Duke of Somerset, had been an extremely rich man; but she was also of the blood royal, a great-granddaughter of John of Gaunt, Duke of Lancaster, third son of the all too prolific King Edward III.

It is not likely that anyone thought of seeking Lady Mar-garet's views on these new arrangements for her future. Mar-riages in royal and noble families were made not in heaven but

7

at the council table, with political or dynastic advantage in mind, and frequently planned when those most closely concerned were still of nursery age. Margaret herself was already contracted to John de la Pole, son of her former guardian the Duke of Suffolk, and being a pious, serious-minded child, the thought of breaking a promise made before God caused her a good deal of heart searching.

According to the story repeated many years later by her close friend John Fisher, Bishop of Rochester, 'being not yet fully nine years old and doubtful in her mind what she were best to do, she asked counsel of an old gentlewoman whom she much loved and trusted'. This lady advised her to pray for guidance to St Nicholas, the patron and helper of all true maidens, and, says Fisher, a marvellous thing occurred. That same night, as he had often heard Lady Margaret tell, while she lay in prayer, calling on St Nicholas, whether sleeping or waking she could not be sure, 'about four o'clock in the morning one appeared to her arrayed like a bishop, and naming unto her Edmund Tudor, bade her take him as her husband'.

Margaret's doubts having thus been resolved by the highest authority and the technical impediment of her prior engagement to John de la Pole dealt with by the canon lawyers, the way was clear for what was to turn out to be one of the most fateful weddings in English history. It took place some time in 1455, as soon as the bride had reached the mature and marriageable age of twelve, but whether or not this unusual pairing was a personally happy one is not recorded. Certainly it was brief, for Edmund Tudor died early in November of the following year. Some three months later, on 28 January 1457, his widow, still not quite fourteen years old, gave birth to a son at Pembroke Castle, stronghold of her brother-in-law Jasper.

The first Henry Tudor, so all the chroniclers agree, was a puny infant, and his earliest biographer, Bernard André, gives much of the credit for his survival to his mother's devoted care. But although the young Countess of Richmond was not, like so many of her contemporaries, destined to see her baby die in his cradle, the repercussions of that murderous family quarrel, conveniently known to history as the Wars of the Roses, were soon to separate mother and child. Things had begun to go very badly for the House of Lancaster, and by the spring of 1461 there was a Yorkist king on the throne. By the autumn, Pembroke Castle and with it Margaret Beaufort and her son were in Yorkist hands, and not long afterwards the wardship of five-year-old Henry had been sold to the Yorkist Lord Herbert of Raglan.

Although it is unquestionably a hard thing for any mother to be parted from her child, it was not an especially unusual occurrence in Margaret Beaufort's world, and she would have had no choice but to acquiesce. At least she had the consolation of knowing that her son would be 'honourably brought-up', since the Herberts were thinking of him as a possible husband for their daughter Maud, and she no doubt made sure of receiving regular reports of his progress. She herself re-married about this time to Henry Stafford, a son of the Duke of Buckingham and yet another descendant of Edward iii. Whether or not there was any element of personal choice in this marriage is something else we don't know, but obviously it was necessary. A wealthy young woman could not do without male protection, and Jasper Tudor, that loyal and active supporter of the Lancastrian cause, was now a wanted man.

Margaret's second marriage lasted about ten years, but there were no more children. One chronicler was later to feel that it was 'as though she had done her part when she had borne a man-child, and the same a kynge of the realms'. Perhaps a more likely explanation may be found in the physical effect of parturition on a pubescent girl. Whatever the reason, Margaret never conceived again, and all her life her precious only son was to fill the centre of her universe; all the force of her strong, vital nature being concentrated single-mindedly on the desire for his 'glory and well-doing'. But it was to be many years before any of her dreams came true, and at one time it seemed as if the separation of mother and son might well be permanent.

There was a brief resurgence of Lancastrian fortunes at the beginning of the 1470s, but the so-called 'Readeption' of Henry

VI lasted less than six months, and the battle of Tewkesbury, fought in May 1471, ended in what looked like final disaster for the Red Rose. Almost overnight young Henry Tudor, now in his fifteenth year, had become the sole surviving representative of the House of Lancaster, 'the only imp now left of Henry VI's blood', and therefore liable at any moment to become the object of his Yorkist cousins' unfriendly interest. Fortunately Jasper, tough, resourceful and apparently bearing a charmed life, was at hand to spirit the boy away. Uncle and nephew sailed from Tenby on 2 June and reached a precarious haven in Brittany.

For Margaret Beaufort, who had seen the extinction of her family in the slaughter at Tewkesbury and was now cut off from all communication with her son, the next twelve years must surely have been the bleakest period of her life. True, Henry had escaped and had found sanctuary of a sort, but even in Brittany he was not necessarily safe from the long arm of the triumphant Yorkists. There was at least one attempt to bribe his Breton hosts to give him up, and any sudden shift in international pressures could easily result in his expulsion and death. If he survived, it seemed as if the best that could be hoped for was that one day the House of York would feel sufficiently secure to allow him to come home and enjoy his father's confiscated earldom. Time passed and Edward IV proved a popular and successful king, with two young sons to ensure the continuation of his line. For the exile in Brittany there was nothing to do but wait and hope, while at home his mother waited and prayed. Then, suddenly, everything changed.

At Easter 1483 King Edward died, probably as the result of a cerebral haemorrhage, leaving the thirteen-year-old Prince of Wales to succeed him. Within a matter of weeks the King's brother Richard, Duke of Gloucester, had seized power, declared his two nephews to be illegitimate and confined them both in the Tower for safe-keeping. By June Richard had been crowned and Henry Tudor had become the rival claimant.

We know very little about the ins and outs of the conspiracy woven in favour of the Tudor claim during that summer, but one thing is certain and that is that Margaret Beaufort was one of its instigators. Married now for the third and last time to Thomas, Lord Stanley, head of a powerful Yorkist family and steward of the royal household, she was close to the centre of affairs, and it is tempting to speculate that she may have been among the first to hear the whispers that the princes in the Tower had been murdered by the new king's hired assassins. Certainly there would have been very little chance for Henry as long as Edward IV's sons were alive, and whatever the real truth of the matter, it is not disputed that after midsummer no one outside the Tower ever saw either of the children alive again. By the autumn it was being freely rumoured that they were dead, but by that time Margaret's plans were already in an advanced state of preparation.

Her first step had been to enlist the support of another woman, the widowed queen, Elizabeth Woodville. Edward IV had broken with royal tradition by marrying for love (or, as some said, because the lady was not otherwise available) and socially very much beneath him. The marriage caused considerable ill-feeling at the time and was to give rise to a smouldering resentment among the older nobility and other members of the House of York, who frankly regarded the Queen's numerous relations as a tribe of rapacious upstarts. Elizabeth herself was never liked. She seems to have had an unhappy talent for making enemies, but her reputation for cold-hearted, calculated greed may not be entirely deserved. In a world where it was every man (and woman) for himself, she can hardly be blamed for taking full advantage of her amazing good luck in catching and holding Edward's notoriously roving eye.

Now, in the summer of 1483, her luck seemed to have run out. Apart from the tragic loss of her sons, her marriage had been declared invalid and she had been insulted and stripped of her dower rights by the new king. She and her five daughters were holed up in sanctuary at Westminster when Margaret Beaufort opened negotiations, using as emissary a Welsh physician named Lewis who, by a fortunate coincidence, also attended the Queen. The proposition brought by Lewis was for a marriage between one of the Yorkist princesses – preferably the eldest, another Elizabeth – and Henry Tudor. In return, the Queen would promise the support of the Woodville clan in Henry's bid for power.

The advantages of such a match from the Tudor point of view were obvious. The inclusion of the Yorkist heiress in the new Lancastrian–Tudor claim should go a long way towards satisfying those Yorkists who were already becoming disenchanted with King Richard and alarmed at his ruthlessness. As well as this, any alliance which offered a reasonable prospect of bringing the two factions together and putting an end to the destructive and tedious quarrel which had over-shadowed English political life for so long would be sure of a welcome from the business community, and indeed from all that solid middle section of the population with a vested interest in stability and the maintenance of law and order.

Elizabeth Woodville was ready to co-operate – naturally enough, since Margaret Beaufort's suggestion brought her not only a glimmer of hope for the future but also a possibility of revenge – but the two mothers could do nothing without money and men. Fortunately Margaret at least was not short of money or of the means of raising it, and she had begun to employ her trusted steward, Reginald Bray, on the delicate task of canvassing support for her project among 'such noble and worshipful men as were wise, faithful and active'. She'd also been doing a little canvassing of her own. Some time that summer, as the Lady Margaret was travelling from Bridgnorth on a pilgrimage to the shrine of Our Lady of Worcester, she happened to encounter the Duke of Buckingham on his way to Shrewsbury and, so the story goes, at once took the opportunity of begging him to intercede with the King on her son's behalf, for she earnestly desired that he might be allowed to come home. It's not likely that Buckingham misunderstood this touching maternal plea, made on the excuse of the close blood tie between them (the Duke had been the nephew of Margaret's second husband and was a Beaufort on his mother's side). At any rate

according to the traditional account, it was shortly after this
convenient wayside meeting that he decided to throw his very
considerable weight behind the unknown quantity of Henry
Tudor. This was a curious decision for a man who, until very
recently, had been one of Richard of Gloucester's strongest supporters and who could himself have made quite a convincing
bid for the throne. But then, if we knew what actually passed
between Margaret Beaufort and Henry Stafford on the road
from Bridgnorth to Worcester that summer day, we should
know a great deal more about the intense personal and political
manœuvring which preceded the change of dynasty.

Couriers bearing news, instructions and large sums of cash
were now slipping unobtrusively across to Brittany, while Margaret waited for her son to justify her unswerving faith in him.
But she was playing a dangerous game. Before the end of September the King had got wind of what was going on, and by
the middle of October the *coup* had collapsed. The Duke of
Buckingham was captured and executed, and Margaret might
well have suffered a similar fate, had not Richard been reluctant to antagonize the influential Stanley family. This, at least,
is the explanation usually given for the fact that the Lady Margaret escaped the normal punishment of those caught plotting
against the State. Instead, she forfeited her property, which was
transferred to her husband for his lifetime, and Thomas Stanley
was ordered to keep his wife under better control in future,
removing her servants and making sure that she could not pass
any messages to her son or her friends, nor practise against the
King. All this, says Polydore Vergil, was done, but although
Margaret's outside activities might have been curtailed, she
continued to work on her husband, and when at last Henry
landed in South Wales in August 1485, he was pretty well
assured of the Stanleys' support. This was of great importance,
as the family owned vast estates in Cheshire and the West
Midlands, and while admittedly they waited until the last
possible moment before committing themselves, it was the
Stanleys' intervention which turned the scales at the battle of
Bosworth.

Unfortunately we have no record of the first meeting between mother and son after the triumph of Bosworth, but it seems reasonable to assume that it was not long delayed. Certainly Henry Tudor showed a very proper recognition of the enormous debt he owed his mother. Thomas Stanley was rewarded with the earldom of Derby, and the first Tudor Parliament restored to Margaret Beaufort, Countess of Richmond and Derby, the estates confiscated two years before. As well as this, she was granted the wardship of young Edward Stafford, son and heir of her late ally the Duke of Buckingham, and a life interest in numerous manors and lordships. The Parliament of 1485 also conferred upon her the rights and privileges of a 'sole person, not wife nor covert of any husband', thus giving her control of her huge fortune 'in as large a form as any woman now may do within the realm'. 'My lady the King's mother', as she was usually styled, had therefore become an extremely rich and important personage, allowed to sign herself Margaret R and, for all practical purposes, honorary Queen Dowager. Bearing in mind the vital biological and political part she had played in establishing the new dynasty, this seems fair enough but, as far as Margaret was concerned, it's probably safe to say that her real reward had been the moment when she saw 'her son the King crowned in all that great triumph and glory'. Her friend John Fisher was to recall how she wept copiously throughout the ceremony, explaining that 'she never was yet in that prosperity, but the greater it was the more she dreaded adversity'. It was a natural reaction after all those years of anxiety, disappointment and fear, but there was to be no more adversity for Margaret Beaufort, and three months later she saw another of her long-cherished plans come to fruition. On 18 January 1486 Henry Tudor fulfilled the pledge he had given in the aftermath of the abortive *coup* of 1483 and married Elizabeth, King Edward's daughter – a union which all sensible people devoutly hoped would mark the end of the Wars of the Roses.

Elizabeth of York, another woman to whom the Tudor dynasty owes a large debt of gratitude, was not quite twenty-one at the time of her marriage – an unusually advanced age for a king's daughter to be still unwed. As a child, Elizabeth had been betrothed to the King of France, but this arrangement had fallen through, and her father's death, followed by the upheavals of the Gloucester take-over, had drastically affected her prospects.

If it was accepted that a hereditary title could be transmitted through the female line (and Henry Tudor's hereditary title, such as it was, devolved entirely from his mother), then the Yorkist branch of the Plantagenet tree was the senior and, as Edward IV's eldest surviving child, Elizabeth's claim to be queen in her own right was infinitely stronger than Henry's to be king. There was nothing in English law to prevent a woman from occupying the throne, but in the political climate of the late fifteenth century such an idea would obviously have been unthinkable, and there is no evidence that the Yorkist heiress herself ever resented the subordination of her rights to the Lancastrian claimant. Indeed, according to a contemporary ballad, *The Most Pleasant Song of Lady Bessy*, Elizabeth, horrified at the thought of being forced into marriage with her uncle Richard, summoned Lord Stanley and begged him to help the exiled Henry to come home and claim his right. When Stanley hesitated – he was afraid of Richard and besides it would be a deadly sin to betray his King – Bessy flung her headdress on the ground and tore her hair 'that shone as the gold wire', while 'tears fell from her eyes apace'. Lord Stanley was touched by her distress, but still he hung back. 'It is hard to trust women,' and Bessy might let him down. He also protested, rather feebly, about the difficulties of communicating with Henry. He himself cannot write and dare not confide in a secretary. But dauntless Lady Bessy was ready for him. She can read and write, if necessary in French and Spanish as well as English, and she will act as scrivener. Deeply impressed by the talents of this 'proper wench', Stanley gave in and, late that night, alone together in Bessy's chamber and fortified by wine and spices, they concocted a series of letters to Stanley's friends and to 'the Prince of England' in Brittany. It was Bessy who found a trusty messenger, Humphrey Brereton, and she was presently rewarded by a love letter from Henry, telling her that he will travel over the sea for her sake and make her his queen.

The Song of Lady Bessy, which was probably written by Humphrey Brereton, a squire in the Stanley household, contains a number of authentic touches and a good deal of poetic licence. All the same, it's quite possible that Elizabeth may have been in touch with Henry at some point in the months before Bosworth and may have sent him a message of encouragement by one of the secret couriers going over to France. Although she had never seen him, she would, of course, have heard glowing reports from Margaret Beaufort, and in any case – whether or not there was ever any truth in the story that King Richard was contemplating marrying his niece – Elizabeth of York seems to have come to the conclusion that a Tudor triumph offered the best hope of a secure and honourable future that she could reasonably expect.

Henry has often in the past been accused of deliberately delaying his wedding in order to forestall any suggestion that he owed the throne to his wife, but although the marriage was certainly of great political importance, the new King's title could in no way be strengthened by his wife's. It was the second generation of Tudor monarchs which would benefit from this union of 'the two bloodes of high renowne', and Elizabeth's real usefulness would depend quite simply on her fecundity. The Yorkist princess had been rescued from the power of her wicked uncle, and the reproach of bastardy, laid on her by Richard's government, had been removed by act of Henry's first Parliament. She had been raised to the dignity of queen consort. Her mother had been rehabilitated and her sisters suitably settled. In return she was expected to be fruitful and thus ensure the future of the new royal line. By contemporary standards, it was a perfectly fair bargain.

There can be no question that Elizabeth understood her historic role, and she was to fill it nobly. She became pregnant immediately, and in September 1486 her first child, Prince Arthur, 'the Rosebush of England', was born a month prematurely at Winchester amid universal relief and rejoicing. There was a gap of three years before another living child arrived, a daughter christened Margaret, whose dynastic value was to equal that of the grandmother for whom she was named. Eighteen months later came another son, Henry, and the following year, 1492, another daughter, Elizabeth. A third daughter, Mary, was born in March 1495, and a third son, Edmund, in February 1499.

The King's mother had retired from political life once her object had been achieved, and, while her daughter-in-law was occupied with the all-important business of filling cradles, Margaret Beaufort turned her attention and her considerable organizational talents to domestic matters, laying down a series of Ordinances designed to ensure the smooth running of the royal household. Like most grandmothers, she was greatly concerned with the welfare of her grandchildren, but this grandmother had more reason than most to take a keen interest in the continuance and well-being of the family she had founded, and the first of her directives covered the preparations to be made 'against the deliverance of a queen'.

As soon as the mother-to-be had decided where she wished the event to take place, a suite of rooms must be got ready and 'hanged with rich arras'. The lying-in chamber itself was to be completely hung with tapestry, walls, ceiling and windows, 'except one window, which must be hanged so as she may have light when it pleaseth her'. The floor was to be 'laid all over and over with carpets' and a royal bed installed. The 'furniture appertaining to the Queen's bed' included a mattress stuffed with wool, a feather bed and a bolster of down. The sheets were to measure four yards broad by five yards long, and there must be two long and two square pillows stuffed with fine down. The counterpane should be of scarlet cloth, furred with ermine and trimmed with crimson velvet and rich cloth of gold; while the whole outfit was to be garnished with silk fringe in blue, russet and gold and topped with crowns embroidered in gold and, of course, the royal arms. Luxury on this scale was naturally beyond the reach of the average family, but every household, excepting the very poorest, could provide a feather pillow and some additional comforts for the woman in childbed.

My lady the King's mother went on to describe the procedure to be followed when the Queen 'took her chamber' – that is when she retired from public gaze, usually about a month before the actual birth. After hearing divine service in a chapel 'well and worshipfully arrayed' for the occasion, she would hold a reception in her 'great chamber' for the lords and ladies of the Court, and the company would be served with wine and spices. After this, the two lords of highest rank present would escort her to the door of the inner chamber and there take leave of her. 'Then', wrote Lady Margaret, 'all the ladies and gentlewomen to go in with her, and none to come into the great chamber but women; and women to be made all manner of officers, as butlers, panters, sewers, etc.' From now on, everything needful would be brought to the outer door of the great chamber and there received by the women officers.

Again, this sort of elaborate ceremonial was reserved for royal and noble households, but in every stratum of society childbirth was regarded as an exclusively female affair. When the *accoucheur*, or man-midwife as he was rather scornfully referred to, began to make his appearance during the seventeenth and eighteenth centuries, he met with considerable hostility from more conventional midwives, who furiously resented this encroachment on their preserves.

At Court the great ladies of the realm gathered as of right to attend the Queen through her ordeal, but in every walk of life a lying-in was a social occasion when all the neighbourhood wives would assemble to 'make good cheer' and support and encourage the woman in labour. The knowledge that the party could so easily end in tragedy doesn't appear to have dampened anyone's spirits. Death was, after all, an everyday occurrence and physical pain an integral part of everyone's experience.

Assuming things went well, the next event to be provided for was the christening and this normally took place within a few days of birth – infant life was too uncertain to permit of any unnecessary delay. A royal christening was a state occasion, with the church lavishly decorated throughout and the necessary lords spiritual and temporal in attendance. Lady Margaret noted that these personages, plus those appointed to be godparents or gossips, should be lodged near the place where the Queen was delivered so that they would be ready and waiting to accompany the young prince or princess to church. In pre-Reformation days, it was customary to immerse the naked infant in the font, so a screened 'travers', or closet, must be prepared with a 'fair pan of coals', plenty of cushions and carpets and a supply of warm water, where the baby could be undressed and if necessary washed – whatever happened, he must not catch cold. After the baptism – and with her unremitting eye for detail Margaret Beaufort decreed that the font must be well raised, so that the congregation would have a good view of the proceedings and not be tempted to press too close – a lighted taper was put into the child's hand and it was carried to the high altar to be confirmed by the officiating bishop. 'All which solemnities accomplished,' it was returned to the travers to be dressed again, while the godparents were served with refreshments and the christening gifts presented. Then the procession formed up again and the newly-christened prince or princess, carried by a duchess, was brought home 'in such sort as it was carried to the church, saving that the torches must be lighted, and a cloth of estate borne over it'. The christening gifts were delivered to the Queen, and the baby was brought in to receive her blessing before being taken back to the nursery. Parents were not much in evidence at a christening. This was the godparents' occasion, and, in any case, the mother was scarcely in a condition to leave her bed.

Lady Margaret's concern for her grandchildren did not end with baptism, and she laid down careful rules for the management of the royal nursery. There was to be a Lady Governess or Lady Mistress to supervise the wet nurse and the dry nurse, who had under them three assistant nurses or cradle rockers. The loyalty and reliability of these intimate personal attendants was vitally important, and their oaths of service were therefore to be administered by the Chamberlain of the Household in person, while the yeomen, grooms and other lesser servants who waited on the nursery must all be sworn 'in the most straitest manner'.

A key member of the nursery staff was, of course, the wet nurse, who must be healthy, clean in her person and habits and of unimpeachable character, for it was generally believed that an infant imbibed its nurse's morals or lack of them along with her milk. The royal wet nurse was a privileged person, and her food and drink were assayed (that is, tasted as a precaution against poison) 'during the time that she giveth suck to the child'; but Lady Margaret insisted that there should be a physician on duty to oversee her at every feed to make sure she was doing her job properly and not adding any unsuitable titbits to her charge's diet. The habit of employing a wet nurse was by no means confined to royal circles – most city-dwellers who could afford to do so would put their babies out to nurse in the country, hoping they might stand a better chance of survival away from the stench and noise and general nastiness of the streets. Wet nurses, incidentally, were sometimes used to nourish the old and toothless as well as the young and toothless – a somewhat gruesome but undeniably practical arrangement.

The royal babies spent most of their time in a wooden cradle, a yard and a quarter long and twenty-two inches broad, lying under a scarlet coverlet furred with ermine. The nursery equipment also included a 'great cradle of estate', much larger and more imposing and heavily encrusted with silver and gilt, in which the latest infant could be shown off to visitors. But in her list of 'necessaries as belong unto the child', Margaret Beaufort did not overlook such humble items as 'a great pot of leather for water' and 'two great basins of pewter' for the baby's washing and, of course, the usual quantities of soft furnishings – curtains, wall-hangings, carpets and cushions – all intended to help keep out the icy draughts which whistled through the grandest houses.

Despite the anxious care lavished on Henry VII's children, my lady the King's mother, her son and daughter-in-law were to know the sorrow of seeing the little Princess Elizabeth die at three years old and Prince Edmund at sixteen months; while there was at least one other child, a boy, born alive, who did not survive to be named. Death which preyed on babies, often in the shape of some form of enteritis, was no respecter of rank or dignity.

During the early years of the reign, Lady Margaret was much in evidence at her son's Court. We know she was present at Winchester for the birth and christening of her first grandchild. She was there to see Henry's triumphant entry into London after his victory at Stoke in November 1487 – strictly speaking the last battle of the Wars of the Roses. She was present at Queen Elizabeth's coronation and at most of the elaborate feasts and shows with which Henry Tudor was at pains to impress the world at large and demonstrate that the new dynasty had come to stay.

Politically, of course, Margaret was still valuable – the sight of her tall, stately, coroneted figure accompanying the King and Queen at public functions serving to remind people that Henry was no mere upstart, that the blood of Edward III and 'time honour'd Lancaster' flowed in his veins too. On the more personal side, there's no reason to suppose that my lady the King's mother was not human enough to be enjoying herself and, in a dignified way, revelling in the sight of her beloved son's continuing success. It's true that some unkind people hinted that the Queen was being deliberately pushed into the background but, although Elizabeth of York may sometimes have found her formidable mother-in-law a trifle overpowering, there's no evidence to suggest that relations between the two ladies were ever anything but affectionate.

In any case, Margaret Beaufort had many other preoccupations which, as time went by, took up more and more of her attention. As well as actively supervising the complicated business of administering her own vast estates (and she never hesitated to resort to litigation in defence of her just rights), she was responsible for the equally enormous possessions of her ward, the young Duke of Buckingham: a responsibility which must have been faithfully discharged, since the Duke counted as one of the richest men in England when he reached his majority. Buckingham and his younger brother were brought up in Lady Margaret's household, where, according to the usual custom, she established a little school of handpicked companions to share their education, and in 1493 wrote to the Chancellor of the University of Oxford asking leave of absence for one Maurice Westbury whom she wished to employ as their tutor.

The list of her charitable works and benefactions is a long one. 'Poor folk to the number of twelve she daily and nightly kept in her house, giving them lodging and drink and clothing, visiting them often, and in their sickness comforting them and administering to them with her own hands, records John Fisher; but probably Margaret Beaufort is best remembered for her patronage of the University of Cambridge where, guided by Fisher, himself a Cambridge man, she made generous endowments to the newly re-founded Christ's College and herself founded St John's.

But although Margaret was a highly intelligent and literate woman – she had been well grounded in French and often regretted she had not made more of her opportunities to study Latin – her interest in such matters never extended to promoting higher education for girls. She encouraged the printer Wynkyn de Worde to bring out books of devotion in the vernacular but remained largely untouched by the rising tide of questing intellectual excitement beginning to sweep through Christendom. Her purpose in founding colleges and endowing readerships was simply that the universities should have the means of adequately performing their primary task of training an efficient and well-educated clergy. Always devout, Lady Margaret commonly spent several hours of each busy day in prayer and meditation, hearing four or more Masses on her knees, and before she went to bed at night never failed 'to resort to her chapel and there for a large quarter of an hour to occupy her devotions'. Always a sparing eater, she observed fast days meticulously and during Lent would restrict herself to one fish meal a day. According to John Fisher, she was also in the habit of wearing a hair shirt or girdle on certain days of every week 'when she was in health'. The author of the Italian *Relation of the Island of England* noted that many Englishwomen carried long rosaries in their hands and that those who could read would take the Office of Our Lady to church with them, reciting it verse by verse with a companion; but although most of her contemporaries were careful in the outward observance of their religious duties, Lady Margaret's piety was deeply-felt devotion on a grand scale. Next to her son, her religion was undoubtedly the most important thing in her life.

As she grew older and more and more immersed in her various charitable and business affairs, my lady the King's mother was seen less often at Court, but she seldom missed any big family occasion. Certainly she was in town in November 1501 for the wedding of Arthur, Prince of Wales, and the Spanish Princess Catherine of Aragon. Once again she 'wept marvellously' throughout the splendid ceremony in St Paul's Cathedral, but this time, unhappily, Lady Margaret's perennial dread that adversity would follow triumph proved well founded, for within six months Arthur was dead at the age of fifteen.

The loss of their precious elder son and heir came as a terrible blow to his parents, and we have a poignant glimpse of Queen Elizabeth attempting to comfort her husband, reminding him that his mother 'had never no more children but him only and that God had ever preserved him and brought him where he was'. They still had a fair prince and two fair princesses, and there might yet be more. 'We are both young enough', said Elizabeth gallantly. She was now in her thirty-eighth year and after seven pregnancies could reasonably have felt she had more than done her duty in this respect, but it seems that for Henry's sake she was ready to begin all over again if necessary – a gesture which in itself suggests a bond of tender affection, if not real love between them.

Meanwhile the three surviving children were growing up, and January 1502 had seen the betrothal of Margaret, elder of the two fair princesses, to King James IV of Scotland. The ceremony took place at Richmond Palace, Patrick, Earl of

Bothwell, acting as James's proxy, and in the presence of her parents, her brother and sister and a notable assemblage of bishops, lords and ladies, Margaret, 'wittingly and of deliberate mind, having twelve years complete in age in the month of November last past', solemnly plighted her troth, vowing to take 'the said James, King of Scotland, unto and for my husband and spouse, and all other for him forsake during his and mine lives natural'. The trumpeters blew a fanfare, the minstrels struck up 'in the best and most joyfullest manner', and the Queen took her daughter by the hand and led her to the place of honour at a banquet laid out in the royal apartments in recognition of her altered status.

Margaret was now officially regarded as a married woman and addressed in public as Queen of Scotland, but another eighteen months were to pass before she left home, and during that time tragedy struck again at the royal family. In February 1503 Elizabeth of York was brought to bed of her eighth child, a girl christened Katherine, but it killed her, and the baby for whom she had given her life 'tarried but a small season after her mother'.

The Queen had always been a popular figure – 'one of the most gracious and best beloved princesses in the world in her time being' – and she was genuinely mourned. She never took any active part in politics and probably never wanted to, but in her own sphere her influence seems to have been entirely benign. To her contemporaries she embodied all the most admired female virtues, being a chaste, fruitful and submissive wife, a loving mother, a dutiful daughter, an affectionate sister and a pious, charitable Christian. She is said to have been beautiful, and probably she was a pretty woman – the Yorkists were a handsome family, and Elizabeth Woodville must certainly have possessed considerable physical attractions. Fortunately, though, her daughter inherited none of the dowager's less admirable characteristics and, from the scanty personal information available, a picture emerges of what is usually described as a very feminine woman – placid, warm-hearted, sweet-tempered and generous, but naturally indolent, totally without ambition, happy to let others take the lead (and the responsibility) and perfectly content in her own small family world. In the often still dangerously tense political atmosphere, this was precisely what the new dynasty needed, and by her negative as well as her positive qualities Elizabeth of York undoubtedly helped to provide a stabilizing element.

Henry honoured his wife with a splendid state funeral. She was buried in Westminster Abbey, with her sister, Lady Katherine Courtenay, acting as chief mourner, while the King 'departed to a solitary place to pass his sorrow'. The Queen's death, says one account, 'was as heavy and dolorous to the King's highness as hath been seen or heard of', but Henry could not afford the luxury of mourning for long. The daily grind of government had to go on, and that summer the young Queen of Scotland was due to travel north to begin her married life. The King escorted his daughter as far as his mother's house at Collyweston in Northamptonshire, where Margaret Beaufort now spent most of her time, and here the goodbyes were said. The bride was to make the rest of her wedding journey in the charge of the Earl and Countess of Surrey, who would be responsible for handing her over to her husband.

There was no sentimental cult of youth in the sixteenth-century world – life was altogether too short and too uncertain – and few concessions were made to immaturity. Margaret, still three months short of her fourteenth birthday, was admittedly young to be married and a queen, but by no means exceptionally so. Her father, and society at large, regarded her as an adult and expected her to behave as one.

The marriage was, of course, entirely a matter of political convenience, intended to seal a treaty of alliance which, it was hoped, would end the ancient feud between England and her nearest neighbour, loosen the almost equally ancient Franco-Scottish connection – always a source of trouble and danger to England – and secure the vulnerable northern frontier. Henry had been negotiating this treaty for a number of years and regarded its completion as something of a triumph. Such considerations as those that his daughter had never seen her future husband, that he was at least fifteen years older and known to be keeping a mistress, were not felt to be relevant. The King of Scotland was a gentleman, and there was no reason to suppose that he would not treat his wife with proper courtesy and respect. As for Margaret, she was making an honourable marriage, a career for which she had been trained from babyhood, and now it was up to her to make a success of it.

The time, indeed, was approaching when the second generation of royal Tudors would have to take over the family business. The King never really recovered from the shock of losing his elder son and his wife within the space of ten months. He aged visibly after the Queen's death, and his health began to fail. He lived for another six years, but when he died, in April 1509, 'of a consuming sickness', at the age of fifty-two, he was already an old man.

His mother did not long survive her own 'sweet and most dear king' and all her worldly joy. Margaret Beaufort was now in her sixty-sixth year, a considerable age by contemporary standards, but her health, even in her last years, seems to have been better than her son's, for she was still active and kept all her faculties to the end. She came up to London to see her eighteen-year-old grandson crowned, staying in the Abbot's House at Westminster for the occasion, and there, at the beginning of July, she died. Her death, coming in the midst of a hectic round of post-coronation festivities, attracted comparatively little attention, though she was, of course, buried with all proper respect alongside her son and daughter-in-law in Henry VII's Chapel in the Abbey, the new Queen, Catherine of Aragon, seeing to most of the arrangements, and John Fisher, Bishop of Rochester, preaching the funeral sermon at a solemn Requiem Mass.

Fisher did full justice to his old friend's memory. 'She had in a manner all that is praisable in a woman, either in soul or body,' he declared; 'she was of singular wisdom and a holding memory; a ready wit she had to conceive all things, albeit they were right dark. In favour, in words, in gesture, in every demeanour of herself, so great nobleness did appear that what-

ever she spoke or did, it marvellously became her.' Fisher went
on to speak of her generosity, her kindliness and her unfailing
good manners. 'Of marvellous gentleness she was unto all folk,
but specially unto her own, whom she loved and trusted right
tenderly. . . . Merciful also and piteous she was unto such as
were grieved or wrongfully troubled, and to them that were
in poverty or any other misery.' The Bishop felt that the whole
country had reason to mourn her passing:

the poor creatures that were wont to receive her alms . . .; the students
of both the Universities, to whom she was as a mother; all the learned
men of England, to whom she was a very patroness; all the virtuous
and devout persons, to whom she was as a loving sister; . . . all good
priests and clerics, to whom she was a true defendress; all the noble
men and women, to whom she was a mirror, an example of honour;
all the common people of this realm, for whom she was in their causes
a common mediatrix, and took right great pleasure for them.

Fisher, of course, was prejudiced, but even so there is no
doubt that my lady the King's mother was a great lady in the
best sense; deeply conscious of the duties and responsibilities
attached to wealth and high position, and tirelessly conscientious in discharging them. Dignified, gracious and good,
there is no doubt that by her life and work she did much to
establish popular respect and esteem for the royal House she
had founded.

CHAPTER TWO

By God's Grace
Boys Will Follow

The one thing pretty well everyone knows about Henry VIII is that he had six wives – admittedly an unusual achievement for any man and unique among English kings. What is not so often known or remembered is that his first marriage lasted very nearly twenty years and that the other five, none of which lasted longer than three years and two only a matter of months, were all squeezed into the last fourteen years of his life.

Almost the first thing the new King did was to get married, taking as his bride his brother's widow, the Spanish Princess Catherine. Some people, so it was said later, had their doubts about the validity of this marriage between brother and sister-in-law from the beginning, but no one apparently felt strongly enough to register a formal protest. The Pope had, after all, issued the necessary dispensations, and Catherine had been officially betrothed to Henry in the summer of 1503 in order to repair the Anglo-Spanish link broken by Arthur's untimely death. The marriage should have taken place in 1505, as soon as Henry had entered his fifteenth year, but the financial and other difficulties which prevented Catherine's father, Ferdinand of Aragon, from delivering the second half of her dowry, and the general deterioration of relations between England and Spain, had combined to postpone the wedding, it seemed indefinitely.

For Catherine the results of this delay were unhappy. One of the conditions of her second marriage contract had been a renunciation of her dower rights as Arthur's widow. Under English law a widow was normally automatically entitled to a third of her late husband's estate, and, as Dowager Princess of Wales, Catherine should have received a third of the revenues of the principality and also of the duchy of Cornwall and earldom of Chester. As matters stood, however, she had been left financially dependent on her father-in-law until her second marriage took place and, as Henry VII's dislike and suspicion of the slippery Ferdinand grew, her position became progressively more uncomfortable. In 1505 Henry cut off the not very generous allowance he had been making her and closed Durham House, where she had been living with her Spanish household. Henceforward the Princess was obliged to live like a poor relation on the fringes of the Court, pawning her plate and selling off bits of jewellery in order to clothe herself and feed her remaining Spaniards, forced to put up with insolence and neglect from the royal servants, cold-shouldered by the family and growing ever more deeply in debt to the London goldsmiths.

But even in her teens Catherine of Aragon was no nonentity to be intimidated by rudeness or dismayed by loneliness and penury. If the King had been hoping that she would beg to go home and thus give him an excuse for breaking off her engagement, he was disappointed. Courageous, stubborn and proud, Catherine bore a strong resemblance to her dead mother, that redoubtable warrior Queen Isabella of Castile, and like a good soldier she stayed grimly at her post. The English, she told her father, could not break her spirit, and she would rather die than return rejected to Spain.

In 1508, a new Spanish ambassador, shocked and disgusted by the way she was being treated and bogged down in a pettifogging wrangle with the King's Council over whether or not the Princess's remaining plate and jewels could be counted against the unpaid portion of her dowry, believed there was nothing for it but to admit defeat. When Catherine heard about this, she was furious. The ambassador, she wrote home energetically, was a traitor who should at once be recalled and punished.

What would have happened if Henry VII had lived another

year is anybody's guess – the course of English history might well have taken a very different direction. But old Henry died, and young Henry, imperiously thrusting aside all the boring financial obstacles in the way of his marriage, made it plain that he wanted no more delay. Although he had scarcely seen his fiancée since their betrothal, the new King, a lusty, full-blooded and, by all accounts, divinely handsome teenager, was impatient to prove his manhood and his mettle in the nuptial bed. This, at least, is the generally accepted explanation for the sudden, dramatic transformation of Catherine's prospects.

Since the King had set his heart on being crowned with the Queen at his side, there was no time to be lost. The wedding took place quietly on 11 June at the Franciscan church close by Greenwich Palace, and ten days later the Court moved to the Tower to prepare for the recognition procession through the City to Westminster and the coronation.

To Catherine, borne through the cheering crowds in a litter draped with cloth of gold slung between two white palfreys, and wearing one of her new trousseau dresses of white embroidered satin, it must surely have seemed that her troubles were over at last. The handsome prince had come riding to her rescue in the best fairy-tale tradition; patience and virtue had been rewarded, and all she had to do now was live happily ever after.

Certainly, in June 1509, everything appeared to be set fair for the young couple. Catherine, to her credit, had not allowed her recent experiences to embitter her. On the contrary, she had learned some valuable lessons in discretion, self-reliance and self-control and had matured into a serene, thoughtful young woman of much dignity and charm. The five-and-a-half year difference in age – Catherine had been twenty-three the previous December, Henry would not be eighteen until the end of the month – seemed unimportant. It might even be all to the good. The ebullient young King, with his passion for violent sports, for lavishly expensive parties and banquets, for dressing up and showing off, could only benefit from the gently restraining influence of a slightly older wife, and during the early years of the reign the Queen's influence – both personal and political – was a factor to be reckoned with.

For two years of her widowhood, Catherine had acted as her father's officially accredited ambassador at Henry VII's Court, and although she'd been unable to achieve anything either for herself or for her country during her term of office, the experience had, nevertheless, given her a useful insight into the workings of the diplomatic machine. She continued after her marriage to take a serious and well-informed interest in international affairs, and there's no doubt that the youthful Henry leaned heavily on her judgement in matters of foreign policy, listening to and frequently taking her advice.

In the spring of 1513, before leaving for the war with France, he made his wife Governor of the Realm and Captain-General of the home forces – a mark of trust and confidence in her abilities which Catherine amply justified. It was a political cliché that the Scots always attacked England whenever the English were fighting in France, and, on this occasion, no sooner had Henry and his army crossed the Channel than the King of Scots forgot that he was married to the King of England's sister and prepared to invade his brother-in-law's territory. Catherine, left in charge with only a skeleton staff of greybeards to help her, found herself responsible for organizing the defence of the kingdom and was soon energetically immersed in the archaic paraphernalia of raising a citizen army. The overwhelming English victory at Flodden that September was worth more than the capture of a dozen French towns, but the Queen was careful not to crow, tactfully attributing her success entirely to English valour and God's grace. Her task was not yet over, for something must be done quickly to reassure the widowed Queen of Scotland – King James having been one of the casualties of Flodden – and this was not without a little social awkwardness. Books of etiquette, even sixteenth-century books of etiquette, offered no guidance on how to condole with your sister-in-law when her husband had just been killed by the army under your command. Margaret Tudor's marriage had never been a particularly happy one, but now, at not quite twenty-four years old and face to face with the prospect of ruling the turbulent, tribal Scots and trying to safeguard the future of her little son, who had succeeded his father at the age of seventeen months, she was understandably distracted with anxiety. The fact that she was three months pregnant did not make her situation any easier, and Catherine, who was also incidentally pregnant, hastened to send 'comfortable messages' to Edinburgh, promising that if Margaret could only keep the Scots quiet, she would be unmolested and able to count on her brother's protection and support.

Everyone agreed that the Queen had coped remarkably well, and when the King returned home in October, they had such a loving meeting that 'every creature rejoiced'. The marriage was still, on the surface at least, an unusually happy one. Husband and wife shared many interests – both loved music and dancing, both had intellectual tastes, and both were devoutly pious – and if, after four years on the throne, Henry had grown out of his initial dependence, he was still undoubtedly very fond of Catherine. He received visitors in her apartments, read the lastest books with her, planned lavish entertainments, so he said, for her pleasure and had not yet lost the habit of discussing his affairs with her. The Queen seemed, indeed, to have all the virtues of an ideal consort except in one vital department – she could not give her husband a male heir.

The tragic story of Catherine's child-bearing had begun in May 1510 with a still-born daughter. She was pregnant again immediately and on New Year's Day 1511 gave birth to a boy, alive and apparently healthy. The baby was christened Henry amid spectacular rejoicings, and the nation breathed a sigh of relief. But unhappily, rejoicing and relief were premature, for the little Prince lived only seven weeks. This was a dreadful blow, and the Queen, 'like a natural woman, made much lamentation'. She miscarried in the autumn of 1513, and in December 1514 another boy was born, but born dead. It was not until February 1516 that Catherine produced another living child. It was a girl, given the name of Mary at the

Friars' Church at Greenwich where her parents had been married.

Henry took the disappointment philosophically. When, some time that summer, the Venetian ambassador ventured to com-
..iserate with him over the baby's sex, he replied cheerfully enough: 'The Queen and I are both young, and if it is a girl this time, by God's grace boys will follow.' The King showed no sign, so far at any rate, that he was seriously worried about his lack of sons. What Catherine thought we do not know, but, as time passed and no boys, indeed no other living children, followed, she began to devote more and more time and thought to the upbringing and education of her daughter.

The notion that girls could and should be given the opportunity to benefit from the kind of academic training normally reserved for boys was of comparatively recent origin, being a by-product of the so-called Renaissance – that great re-birth of learning and intellectual curiosity which had sprung to life in Italy in the fourteenth and fifteenth centuries and spread slowly but steadily northward. It would be more accurate to call it a re-discovery for, paradoxically, the New Learning, as it became known in England, had its roots in a nostalgia for the past. Like most reformers, the Renaissance scholars wanted to go back to the beginning: to revive the classical culture of the ancient world and, especially as the movement gained strength in northern Europe, to return to the purity of the early Apostolic Church. They sought, in fact, to clear away the accumulated debris of the centuries, so that the fountain-head of knowledge and piety and innocence could once more bubble up clean and uncluttered. They turned to the study of Greek partly to re-discover the pre-Christian philosophers but also to be able to read the Gospels in their original form.

The effects of the Renaissance were first felt in England during the fifteenth century – greatly assisted, of course, by the arrival at Westminster in 1477 of William Caxton and his printing press – but the spread of interest in scholarship was due chiefly to the efforts of a group of men who congregated in London and Cambridge in the early 1500s. These individuals, who

included Desiderius Erasmus, Luis Vives the Spaniard, John
Colet (who founded his famous school at St Paul's in 1509),
Thomas Linacre the physician, William Grocyn the Greek
scholar and Sir Thomas More the lawyer, were all deeply interested in education and anxious to propagate their plans for a
wider and more liberal curriculum in the schools and universities. But Thomas More was the first Englishman seriously to
experiment with the novel idea that girls should be educated
too. This may have been partly due to the fact that he had three
daughters and an adopted daughter but only one son, and was
undoubtedly helped by the fact that the eldest girl, Margaret,
turned out to be unusually intelligent and receptive. She and
her sisters Elizabeth and Cecily, together with their foster-sister
Margaret Gigs, studied Latin and Greek, logic, philosophy and
theology, mathematics and astronomy, and Margaret More,
who presently became Margaret Roper, developed into a considerable and widely respected scholar in her own right.

Erasmus had been sceptical about the wisdom of the experiment, but he was so impressed by the mini-Utopia of his friend's
household – 'Plato's Academy on a Christian footing' as he described it – and by the achievements of the eagerly studious
and formidably virtuous young ladies, that he was quite won
over and predicted that More's example would be imitated far
and wide. In fact, girls like Margaret Roper were to remain
the exception rather than the rule, but Sir Thomas did have
one influential supporter in Queen Catherine who, like Margaret Beaufort before her, was a generous patron of scholars
and who now had a special reason for taking an interest in
female education.

With her memories of her own mother, who had fought her
way to a throne, ruled a turbulent country with cool efficiency,
expelled the last of the Arab rulers from Spain and still found
time to bring up a family of five, Catherine naturally saw nothing especially out of the way in the idea of an English queen
regnant, and she was determined that her daughter should be
thoroughly prepared for the task ahead. In 1523, therefore,
when Mary was seven years old, the Queen asked her compa-

triot, Juan Luis Vives, to draw up a plan of studies for the Princess which would help her to grow both in erudition and virtue.

Vives, like all his contemporaries, laid great stress on maintaining a high moral standard and on the importance of character-forming in education. It followed that only the best and most serious of the classical authors should be allowed in the schoolroom, and anything that savoured of romance, lightness or wantonness was to be avoided like the plague. This was particularly important where girls were concerned, since everyone knew that, being naturally frail and 'of weak discretion', they were more easily led astray and more liable to be corrupted into vice by reading unsuitable storybooks.

In spite of the currently fashionable craze for Greek and the growing use of English as a literary medium, a thorough grounding in Latin remained indispensable, and Vives was emphatic that the Princess should learn from the beginning to use Latin in conversation (though she must, of course, be taught correct pronunciation) and to speak it freely with her tutor and with her fellow pupils. He recommended that she should have three or four carefully chosen companions at her lessons, 'for it is not good to be taught alone'. She should also learn to write fluently in Latin from dictation and to translate from English into Latin. Vives suggested that she should get into the habit of keeping notebooks in which she could jot down useful words and phrases, elegant and unusual words, and any passages from the authors she was reading which took her fancy or struck her as being especially wise and helpful, for, as he sensibly remarked, 'those things stick in the memory which we have written with our own hand, rather than that which is written by another's'. He laid stress on the importance of memory-training. The Princess should exercise her memory daily, 'so that there be no day on which she has not learned something thoroughly'. To begin with, on going to bed at night, she should read carefully two or three times anything which was to be learned by heart 'and on the next morning ask herself for it again'. The rules of grammar, on the other hand, instead of being learned by rote, were better absorbed naturally by the study of suitable authors – Cicero, Seneca, the works of Plutarch, Plato's Dialogues, the epistles of St Jerome and St Augustine, Erasmus's Paraphrases, Thomas More's *Utopia* and a selection of Latin poets, including 'a good part of Horace', were all mentioned in Vives's reading list. Mary was also to read something from the New Testament every day, the passages to be suggested by her tutor.

Where the King and Queen led, other parents in their circle naturally followed, and although the cult of the learned woman never spread far beyond that circle, which, in Queen Catherine's time, included most of the intellectual elite, the principle of educating girls to a higher standard than previously had gained an undeniable social cachet.

Not that the new ideas were universally approved. There was a substantial body of opinion which held that to stuff girls' heads with Latin and Greek was 'neither necessary nor profitable' and might well be actively harmful. Women, and especially young women, were notoriously unstable and apt to become excited by novelty; once given access to classical literature, they would be bound to pick up all sorts of unwholesome, half-digested ideas which would make them 'froward' and discontented, if not worse. The intellectuals might talk a great deal about moral uplift, but once a woman had learned to read in English and in foreign tongues, who was to prevent her from getting hold of love stories, tales of adultery and the heathen goings-on of pagan gods and goddesses – matters which no honest woman ought to know about and all too liable to inflame her stomach and distract her from her household duties.

The scholars, of course, argued that the educated woman would inevitably become more serious-minded, a more rational companion for her husband, a better mother to her children. Women were reasonable creatures, and, if they were given the opportunity of improving themselves, their natural tendency to frivolity would be checked. The educated woman, who spent her leisure time in studying instead of idle gossip with her neighbours, was more likely to prove virtuous and chaste than her uneducated counterpart with nothing better to think about than the latest fashion or the latest piece of scandal.

As far as household duties were concerned, it is noticeable that not even the most advanced educational theorist ever dreamed of challenging society's two basic assumptions – that a woman's place was in the home and that the nice girl's only ambition should be to make an honourable marriage and become a good wife and mother. Indeed, the educational theorists from Luis Vives downwards all attached great importance to the housewifely arts.

Vives himself was insistent that girls should learn to spin and weave, citing the example of numerous industrious classical and scriptural heroines. The handling of wool and flax were, in his opinion, two crafts yet left of the old innocent world, and he would 'in no wise that a woman should be ignorant of those feats that must be done by hand, no, not though she be a princess or a queen'. He also thought it essential that every girl should learn to cook, to be able to dress meat for her family and 'not lay all the labour upon the servants'. She should take pains to become skilled in invalid cookery. 'I have seen in Spain and in France', he wrote, 'those that have mended of their sickness by meats dressed of their wives, daughters or daughters-in-law, and have ever after loved them far the better for it.' He added, ominously, that women who could not cook were in danger of being hated by their menfolk.

The cheerful conviction that woman had been created for the benefit and domestic comfort of man and that the whole of a girl's education, both formal and practical, should properly be directed to that end, lay not very far beneath the teachings of every sixteenth-century educationist. Richard Mulcaster, a strong believer in book learning for young maidens, wrote: 'I think it and know it to be a principal commendation in a woman: to be able to govern and direct her household, to look to her house and family, to provide and keep necessaries ... to know the force of her kitchen', and he went on to say that every girl, whatever her station in life, should be taught household management. Mulcaster was supported by the author of yet another manual on the education of young ladies, who declared that:

Our gentlewoman shall learn not only all manner of fine needlework . . . but whatsoever belongeth to the distaff, spindle and weaving: which must not be thought unfit for the honour and estate wherein she was borne. . . . And which is more, to the end that being become a mistress, she shall look into the duties and offices of domestical servants, and see how they sweep and make clean the chambers, hall and other places: make ready dinner, dressing up the cellar and buttery: and that she be not so proud that she should disdain . . . but to be present at all household works.

The pros and cons of higher education for women continued to be earnestly discussed, especially during the first half of the Tudor century, and despite the misgivings of the old-fashioned, there's no doubt that literacy among women in general was on the increase. The numbers of cookery books, books on household management, needlework and related feminine interest subjects, as well as books of advice and pious exhortation to wives which were now coming off the presses, indicated that there must have been a worthwhile market for them. The widening availability and comparative cheapness of the printed word naturally gave special impetus to would-be readers, but, at the same time, as life became slowly but steadily more urbanized and more complicated, the wives and daughters of shopkeepers, merchants, traders and small businessmen of every kind were finding it more and more necessary to be able to write a letter, con a legal document and cast up accounts.

Girls continued to learn the traditional arts of baking and brewing, spinning and weaving, butter- and cheese-making and the concoction of herbal remedies from their mothers, just as they had always done, but the acquisition of more formal skills could present a problem. There's evidence that girls as well as boys attended the scattered chantry and parish schools offering elementary education to the local children, and some grammar schools, too, seem to have admitted girls, at any rate to part of their course, but there were as yet no schools for girls in any recognizable sense. In the early years of the century, of course, parents could still send their daughters to a nunnery to learn French, some Latin, needlework, music and Church history. Considerably later on, the Protestant refugees coming in from France and the Low Countries began to set up academies for young ladies, offering a syllabus of French, sometimes Italian, music, dancing, deportment and needlework. Such establishments, though, were only for the few, and in general an ambitious girl would have to rely on her own resources to get an education, learning from one or other of her parents, from an elder brother, the local parish priest or curate, or from a sympathetic and literate neighbour. Quite a number of wives persuaded their husbands to teach them to read. Higher up the social scale there was the family chaplain, or a young noblewoman might share the services of her brother's tutor.

Another method of obtaining extra advantages for daughters which continued to be popular among upper- and middle-class parents was the practice of 'placing out' – that is of sending a girl away to be brought up and educated in a household better circumstanced than one's own. This habit applied to boys as well as girls – boys apprenticed to a craft lived with their masters' families – and had its origins in the feudal custom of sending a boy to serve as a page in his lord's household as the first step in his progress towards knighthood. But 'placing out' for a girl, even if she paid for her keep by performing some domestic duties or by acting as a 'waiting gentlewoman' to her hostess, meant the chance of acquiring accomplishments and social graces not obtainable at home, and consequently the chance of making a better marriage.

Foreigners regarded this system (which was, of course, the forerunner of the boarding-school system) as yet another instance of English cold-heartedness and general 'want of affection' towards their children. 'If the English sent their children away from home to learn virtue and good manners and took them back again when their apprenticeship was over, they might be excused,' wrote the author of the Italian *Relation* severely; 'but they never return, for the girls are settled by their patrons, and the boys make the best marriages they can.'

The girls themselves seldom complained, especially if they were fortunate enough to be placed in a large, wealthy household. Most of the great families kept up almost regal state, and there would be plenty of social life under their roofs. Supervision, too, was liable to be less strict and opportunities of making friends with other young people of both sexes considerably greater. In fact, for an intelligent girl, eager to improve herself and ready to seize her chances, the possibilities were almost limitless – the career of young Mistress Anne Boleyn being perhaps a classic example of this.

It was naturally the height of every family's ambition to get a pretty and promising daughter accepted as one of the Queen's maids of honour, but unless a girl's rank automatically entitled her to a place in the royal entourage, competition was fierce, and much string-pulling on behalf of hopeful candidates was usually necessary. Sir Thomas Boleyn, however, encountered no difficulty when the time came to introduce his younger daughter into Queen Catherine's household.

A combination of shrewd business acumen and a series of advantageous marriages had, in three generations, transformed the Boleyn family from obscure tenant farmers into well-heeled gentry very much on the up and up. Thomas, a younger son, had come to Court at the turn of the century to make a career in the royal service and had established himself as a useful underling, capable and conscientious, a man who could be trusted to carry out instructions. He was, nevertheless, an ambitious man and, like his father and grandfather before him, had married well – to Elizabeth Howard, a daughter of the Duke of Norfolk, who 'brought him every year a child'. Three of these children survived, George, Mary and Anne, born in 1507.

Thomas Boleyn was a careful father who took a serious interest in his daughters' education, but he had no desire to see them become classical scholars. Nor would he have been impressed by the high-minded theories of Luis Vives, who advocated a Spartan upbringing and almost nunlike seclusion for the well-born maiden. Sir Thomas wanted Mary and Anne to learn to move easily and gracefully in the highest circles and to acquire all the social graces, to speak fluent French, to dance and sing and play at least one instrument, to ride and be able to take part in the field sports which were such an all-absorbing passion with the upper classes, and to become familiar with the elaborate code of courtesy which governed every aspect of life at the top. They must learn how to conduct themselves in the presence of royalty, how to cope with the vast quantities of rich food and drink served at royal banquets, how to avoid the obvious pitfalls lying in wait for a young woman exposed to the temptations of high society while, at the same time, attracting the attention of the right sort of man. Mary and Anne were, in short, to be groomed to make the kind of marriage which would add to the family's aristocratic connections and take the Boleyns another step up the social and financial ladder.

The best place to learn about Court life was, of course, at Court, but before launching his daughters on the London scene, Thomas Boleyn was able to make use of his official contacts to get them the special advantage of a Continental 'finish'. In 1512 he was sent on a diplomatic mission to Brussels and took the opportunity to secure a place for Mary, then probably about twelve years old, in the household of Margaret, Archduchess of Austria and Regent of the Netherlands. Two years later an even better opening appeared. The King's younger sister, the beautiful Mary Tudor, was to be married to the King of France and would be accompanied on her wedding journey by a numerous retinue of English ladies in waiting. What better experience could there be for a young girl, and the indefatigable Sir Thomas retrieved his elder daughter from Brussels and got her accepted into the service of the new Queen. Anne still had to be provided for, but Anne was still a child, living most probably at Hever Castle, the family's Kentish property, and receiving her elementary education from Simonette, her French maid or governess.

As it turned out, Mary Tudor's marriage lasted barely three months. The excitement and physical strain of the wedding and its attendant festivities proved altogether too much for the frail, elderly Louis XII, and he died before the end of the year. By the spring of 1515 Mary Tudor was back in England, but Mary Boleyn stayed in France, transferring her allegiance to Queen Claude, the good dull wife of Louis's heir, the anything but good François I. The French Court was widely regarded as being the centre of European culture and civilization, but it was perhaps hardly the most suitable environment for a nubile teenager, since François was well known for his inability to keep his hands off any woman. 'Rarely did any maid or wife leave that court chaste,' remarked the Sieur de Brantôme, and if there is any truth in the gossip, Mary Boleyn certainly did not. She seems, in fact, to have acquired quite a reputation for being generally available and when she returned to England, the finished product of her courtly training, she became Henry VIII's mistress.

Meanwhile it was time to send Anne across the Channel, and this probably took place in 1519, when Sir Thomas Boleyn was appointed ambassador to France. Arrangements were made for twelve-year-old Anne to join the school for young ladies person-ally supervised by Queen Claude, in which that much-tried lady did her utmost to maintain a high moral tone and where, it was to be hoped, moral danger would be avoided. Writing to his younger daughter to inform her of her good fortune, Sir Thomas solemnly enjoined her to be of virtuous repute when she came to Court, to work hard at her French and spelling and generally to make the most of her opportunities on pain of losing his affection of goodwill to advance her interests. Anne's reply, written, she assured him, entirely without help from Simonette, promises her best endeavours and expresses a very proper gratitude and readiness to be ordered by her father in all things. Gratitude and obedience were attributes highly prized by parents, and Thomas Boleyn kept the letter carefully among his papers.

While in France 'Monsieur Boullan's' daughter was noted for her skill in music and dancing and 'all games fashionable at Courts', as well as for her excellent taste in dress – at least so it was remembered afterwards. Whether or not she contrived to keep her virginity, we do not know, but Anne was always far more intelligent and considerably stronger-minded than her sister. Her stay with Queen Claude was curtailed by the breaking off of Anglo-French relations in the autumn of 1521. All English nationals were recalled, and by Christmas she was back at home again. Although she was still only fourteen, her father made no attempt to place her at another European Court, chiefly, it may be assumed, because he already had a husband in mind for her.

Thomas Boleyn's father had married into the noble Anglo-Irish family of Butler, and his mother, Margaret had been the daughter and, with her sister, co-heir of the last earl of Ormonde. A second cousin, Piers Butler, was now laying claim to the vacant earldom, and a promising feud over the rents and revenues of the Ormonde estates had begun to burgeon between the Butlers and the Boleyns. Quarrels of this kind were by no means uncommon among landed families, but this particular quarrel also had political implications, since the goodwill of the Butler clan was of considerable importance to the English government in maintaining the always precarious stability of tribal Ireland. So when someone suggested that the matter might be amicably resolved by a marriage between Thomas Boleyn's daughter and Piers Butler's son, James, the King and Cardinal Wolsey took up the idea with enthusiasm. In the circumstances it is not surprising that Thomas Boleyn had no difficulty in getting his daughter admitted to Queen Catherine's household on her return from France, and Anne made her debut at the New Year revels, dressed in yellow satin and wearing a head-dress of Venice gold.

It is not likely that she had been consulted about the plans being made for her future – neither Thomas Boleyn, with financial and social advantage at stake, nor King and Cardinal, fearing possible trouble in Ireland, would consider the feelings of a fourteen-year-old girl as relevant to the situation – but it's difficult to believe that Anne, that accomplished and sophisticated young lady with a developing taste for the elegancies of

43

life, contemplated the prospect of banishment to an Irish wilderness with any degree of pleasure. Negotiations with the Butlers, though, made slow progress, and in the meantime Anne proceeded to look around on her own account.

As one of the Queen's maids of honour she was, of course, in the best possible position for doing so. The chief function of the maids of honour was to look decorative, to provide a handsome setting for the Queen on all public occasions and generally to ornament the Court. The girls were supposed to occupy their off-duty hours with sewing and serious reading, but inevitably a large proportion of the day was spent in gossiping, playing cards and flirting with the numerous similarly under-employed young gentlemen who were seldom at a loss for an excuse to linger in the Queen's apartments. Among these was Henry Percy, son and heir of the Earl of Northumberland, currently completing his education and seeing something of the great world in the household of Cardinal Wolsey. In the words of George Cavendish, the Cardinal's gentleman usher,

when it chanced the Lord Cardinal at any time to repair to the Court, the Lord Percy would then resort for his pastime unto the Queen's chamber, and there would fall in dalliance among the Queen's maidens, being at the last more conversant with Mistress Anne Boleyn than with any other; so that there grew such a secret love between them that at length they were insured together, intending to marry.

There seems little reason to doubt that young Percy had fallen heavily for the elegant, vivacious brunette with her glamorous aura of foreign travel, but whether Anne was really in love or whether she just found Henry Percy infinitely preferable to James Butler and hoped that her father would regard him as a suitable alternative, we don't know. In either case, her hopes were soon to be blighted, for as soon as word of this promising romance reached the ears of Cardinal Wolsey, he squashed it ruthlessly, scolding the unhappy Percy in front of the servants for his 'peevish folly' in so far forgetting his position and his duty as to become entangled with some foolish little girl at the Court, and forbidding him to see her again on pain of the King's severe displeasure.

George Cavendish, recording the incident in his Life of his master, believed that the King had already begun 'to kindle the brand of amours' for the young lady in question and had ordered Wolsey to intervene. In view of later events, this must have seemed a perfectly reasonable assumption but, in fact, there is no evidence that Henry had any amorous intent towards Anne in 1522, a time when he was probably still enjoying the hospitality of her elder sister's bed. A less romantic but more plausible explanation is that the Cardinal had simply acted to prevent two thoughtless young people from upsetting the plans of their elders and betters. Wolsey and the Earl of Northumberland between them had no difficulty in reducing Lord Percy to an apologetic pulp, but young Anne showed her furious disappointment so plainly that she was sent home in disgrace.

In the autumn of 1522 Thomas Boleyn had little reason to be pleased with either of his daughters. Mary had spoiled her chances by promiscuity, for although there was little real social stigma attached to having been the King's mistress, it undoubtedly affected a girl's matrimonial prospects, and she and her family had a right to expect royal compensation for possible loss of reputation. It's true that Sir Thomas's own career was coming along quite nicely – he'd recently risen to become Treasurer of the Household and was soon to be made a Knight of the Garter – but Henry was notoriously stingy towards his mistresses. Even Elizabeth Blount, who'd presented him with a bastard son, only achieved a respectable marriage, and Mary Boleyn had to be content with William Carey, one of the King's boon companions but otherwise of no particular account. Mary's father may well have reflected gloomily on how much better these things were managed in France, where the *maîtresse en titre* was a public figure wielding influence and patronage who could normally expect to retire on a more than comfortable fortune. As for Anne, it looked as if the child had ruined herself at the outset by her headstrong behaviour and inability to control her temper.

But Anne was to have a second chance. Her rustication seems to have lasted for about three years, and when she returned to Court, at either the end of 1525 or the beginning of 1526, she was still unbetrothed – the Butler marriage had finally fallen through, and there were, it seems, no other suitors under consideration. She was now in her nineteenth year and, to the outward eye, quite unconcerned about the unsettled state of her future. All the same, she must have been well aware that time was passing and very conscious of the fact that she couldn't afford to make any more mistakes. While she waited for something to turn up, Anne had begun to amuse herself by a flirtation with Thomas Wyatt, the witty and talented courtier, poet and diplomat who was a neighbour of the Boleyns down in Kent. She and her brother George and Thomas Wyatt formed a close little clique, gay, brilliant and irreverent, and although we know precious little about the actual inception of the King's grand passion for Mistress Anne, it is at least probable that it was the obvious interest of Thomas Wyatt, himself a married man, which first stirred Henry to take notice of the lady.

The game of courtly love, derived from the mediaeval French romances which were such popular reading, was a recognized pastime in high society. It involved much sighing and languishing and mournful serenading on the part of the young men – much coyness and 'cruelty' on the part of the ladies, whose 'lovers' became their true knights and servants to command. None of this, of course, had anything to do with real life, and as soon as any real feelings were stirred, the conventions of the game rapidly disappeared. Anne seems to have succeeded in keeping the pretence of her 'court' going for several months, but a man like Henry Tudor would not brook competition for long. There was some by-play over a trinket belonging to Anne and flourished by Wyatt during a game of bowls with the King. Henry, in turn, produced a ring which, he declared, she had given to him, and the episode ended with his majesty stumping away in a huff, muttering that he had been deceived. Since all the Boleyns depended heavily on royal goodwill, Anne had hastily to smooth things over, and Thomas Wyatt melted sadly but wisely into the background.

By the late summer of 1526 the whole Court knew that Anne Boleyn was the King's latest inamorata, but no one, at this stage, 'esteemed it other than an ordinary course of dalliance'. There is, in fact, no reason to suppose that, at this stage, the King had anything other than an ordinary course of dalliance in mind, but Anne soon made him understand that she had no intention of becoming his mistress. With the example of her elder sister before her, she knew it would lead to nothing more than a second-rate and perhaps unhappy marriage, and she meant to do better than that. Just when she began to realize that she might, if she played her cards carefully, win herself the greatest matrimonial prize of all, we unfortunately have no means of knowing. Probably it dawned on her gradually during that autumn and winter as the King, unaccustomed to being refused, started to pursue her with ever-increasing fervour, while she withdrew nervously, protesting her virtue and retreating to Hever when the pressure grew too great, but never – as a modest young lady thus honoured by her sovereign could scarcely do – never repulsing him entirely.

Whether this very feminine display was all part of a deliberate cold-blooded plan or whether it proceeded from genuine embarrassment and perplexity in the face of an admittedly awkward dilemma, Anne could not have adopted better tactics, for Henry, in spite of his highly-coloured reputation, was no casual lecher. In a series of letters, undated but almost certainly written during the spring of 1527, he begs repeatedly – almost abjectly – for an unequivocal declaration of her love, offering in return to make her his 'sole mistress' and to reject all others 'out of mind and affection'. Although the sixteenth-century sense of the word 'mistress' did not necessarily imply its modern physical connotation, Anne was taking no chances. She knew her own strength by this time – the King had given himself away too completely – and she would respond to only one kind of suggestion. Just when Henry came to accept this, to decide that here was a woman worthy to be his wife and actually to make that momentous proposal, is something else we don't know. All we do know for certain is that by May 1527 he had taken the first, tentative steps towards obtaining his freedom, without, incidentally, having the courtesy to inform the lady who had been his faithful and devoted consort for very nearly eighteen years, and thus set in motion a train of events which was radically to alter the course of English history.

CHAPTER THREE

The King's Lady

Henry VIII's so-called divorce from his first wife – the King's 'great matter' as it was cautiously referred to by those in the know during its early stages – was to overshadow English foreign and domestic politics for the best part of ten years. Its most immediate and far-reaching consequence, the breach with Rome and the establishment of a national Church, directly affected the lives of every man, woman and child in the country and was to lead to a dangerous isolation from the main body of Christendom – an isolation whose implications became increasingly alarming as the Tudor century unfolded. Many good men, and women too, were to die, many useful lives would be wrecked, and many ancient, revered institutions be overthrown because the King of England wished to take a new wife.

When, in the spring of 1527, the King, so he said, first began to doubt the validity of his marriage to his brother's widow, divorce in its modern sense was unknown. It's true that the Church could, in exceptional cases of flagrant adultery or cruelty, or if one partner became a heretic, be persuaded to grant the equivalent of a judicial separation, but it was generally held that, since 'a man and woman conjoined in matrimony be by God's ordinance but one flesh and body', the marriage bond was indissoluble. In the years immediately following the Reformation, there were isolated cases of a complete divorce, allowing the innocent party to re-marry, being granted by the ecclesiastical authorities with royal approval, but on the whole, by the end of Elizabeth's reign, divorce had become more and not less difficult to obtain, and in 1602 the door was finally shut.

The ending of a marriage by a decree of nullity, pronouncing the contract void from the beginning, was a different matter and, although normally beyond the reach of ordinary people, was neither particularly difficult nor even particularly unusual among the great and the powerful with money and influence at their disposal. There were a number of grounds on which an annulment could be applied for, including misrepresentation, whether deliberate or not, regarding the status – social, financial or marital – of either party at the time the marriage contract was drawn up; forced matrimony, alleging that the consent of either or both parties had not been freely given; pre-contract, when one of the parties had already promised, before witnesses, to marry another; the impotence, madness or taking of a formal vow of chastity by one of the parties; and consanguinity or affinity, where it could be shown that husband and wife were related, either by blood or marriage, within one of the prohibited degrees.

Henry's famous 'scruple of conscience' – his fear that he might, unwittingly of course, have been living in sin all those years – was based on a text in the Book of Leviticus which stated uncompromisingly that 'if a man shall take his brother's wife, it is an unclean thing ... they shall be childless'. This, the King realized in an apparently blinding flash of revelation, must be the reason for his hitherto inexplicable failure to beget a male heir. The more he thought about it, the more convinced he became that the Queen's inability to bear a living son must surely be a sign of God's displeasure at their unlawful cohabitation. Why else should the deity, who had always shown such a flattering degree of interest in his doings, deny him male children? Having thus come to the convenient conclusion that he was, after all, still a bachelor, Henry felt free to pursue his natural inclinations supported by an uplifting sense of moral rectitude. Indeed, so completely satisfied did he appear with the justice of his cause, that one observer believed an angel descending from heaven would have been unable to persuade him otherwise.

Nevertheless, the King could not feel at all certain that his

wife would see the matter in the same light, and he was noticeably uneager to break the news to her. When at last he did
nerve himself to do so, Catherine could find no words to answer
him. It was many years now since she had been her husband's
confidante, had shared his problems and his growing pains and
had been permitted to offer him advice. It was a good many
years, too, since Henry had worn her favour in the lists, had
laid his youthful triumphs at her feet and come hurrying to
bring her any titbits of news he thought would interest or please
her. But although they had grown apart, although other people
had shouldered her out of his confidence, for Catherine, Henry
would always remain the beautiful young man who had rescued
her from lonely humiliation – the gay, generous boy who had
loved her and made her his queen in that long-ago joyous
springtime, when life had been spent in 'continual festival'. She
could accept, though sadly, that love must die, but that the
man whose 'true and humble' wife she had been, whose children she had borne and whose interests she had loyally tried to
serve, was now apparently prepared to discard her, to wipe out
nearly twenty years of married life as though it had never been,
callously to dishonour her name and to bastardize their
daughter, was a betrayal too black for speech. As Catherine
listened to her husband's glib talk of his troubled conscience,
of how they had been in mortal sin during all the years they
had lived together and inviting her to choose a place of retire-
ment away from the Court, words refused to come, and she collapsed into helpless, uncharacteristic tears.

It was a shortlived collapse, and the Queen soon made it
abundantly clear that she intended to fight every inch of the
way. Her position was simple and could be simply stated. If
the King was really worried about the validity of their marriage, then it was right that the matter should be examined and
his doubts laid to rest. As for herself, her conscience was clear,
and she had nothing to fear from a free and impartial enquiry.
She knew that she was, had always been and always would be
Henry's true and lawful wife. Had they not been married in
the sight of God by the Archbishop of Canterbury himself, with

the approval of the wisest men in England and Spain? Her first marriage to the boy Arthur had never been consummated, and she had come to Henry, as she was presently publicly to remind him, 'as a very maid without touch of man'. Therefore, the affinity prohibited in Leviticus did not exist, and Henry need have no qualms about the Pope's power to set aside the law of God.

When the Pope's representative, Cardinal Campeggio, came over to England in 1528 to try to arrange an amicable settlement, he found Catherine immovable in her determination to defend to the last the soul and the honour of her husband and herself. She utterly rejected the suggestion that she should give in gracefully and retire into a nunnery. She had no vocation for the religious life and intended to live and die in the estate of matrimony to which God had called her. But, she told Campeggio, she was an obedient daughter of the Church. She would submit to the Pope's judgement in the matter and abide by his decision, whichever way it might go. Unless and until judgement was given against her, she would continue to regard herself as the King's lawful wife and England's Queen and nothing, declared England's Queen flatly, would compel her to alter this opinion – not if she were to be torn limb from limb. If, after death, she should return to life, she would prefer to die over again rather than change it.

As far as the Pope was concerned, Catherine could scarcely have adopted a more embarrassing position. The Holy Father had no desire to alienate so dutiful a son as the King of England – especially not at a time when the prestige of the papacy was dangerously low – and the King of England was already dropping ominous hints as to what he might do if the case went against him. On the other hand, Catherine had powerful kinsfolk (the Holy Roman Emperor was her nephew) who were well placed to exert pressure on her behalf. The last thing the Pope wanted was to have to pronounce judgement, and during the next six years he made use of every delaying tactic at his disposal to postpone that evil moment. But faced with Henry's urgent impatience, he could not long postpone the initial confrontation, and by the spring of 1529 the legal battle had been fairly joined.

In the manner of most legal battles, it became exceedingly bitter and complicated – and sixteenth-century law governing marriage was complicated enough at the best of times. Henry had taken a fundamentalist stand on Leviticus, but unfortunately there was another passage in the Old Testament, in the Book of Deuteronomy, which ran: 'When brethren dwell together, and one of them dieth without children, the wife of the deceased shall not marry to another; but his brother shall take her, and raise up seed for his brother.' This led to a stimulating international debate among scholars and theologians as to how these two apparently conflicting texts could be reconciled and whether the ancient Jewish law could properly be applied in a Christian community, but it did not help the King to get his divorce. The King's advisers would, in fact, have had an easier time if, unhampered by these scriptural excursions, they could have followed the time-honoured strategy of canon lawyers in such cases and attacked the papal dispensation of 1503 allowing Henry to marry his sister-in-law on the grounds that it had been issued on insufficient or inaccurate information. They could, for example, have pointed out that this dispensation assumed that Catherine's marriage to Prince Arthur *had* been consummated and therefore did not cover the so-called diriment impediment of public honesty, created by the fact that whether or not the marriage had been completed in the sight of God, they had indisputably been through a public wedding ceremony and been married in the sight of the Church. Legal nit-picking perhaps, but the King would have had a much better argument in canon law. Catherine's advisers, too, wished that instead of basing her defence on her virginity at the time of her second marriage – a statement no longer susceptible of legal proof – she had taken her stand on the Pope's undoubted powers to dispense. She could, they reminded her, always apply secretly to Rome for another, supplementary bull, making good any accidental deficiencies in the first.

Unfortunately, though, the King of England's great matter

was based on emotion rather than logic. Behind a smokescreen of legal and theological wrangling, the real battle was being fought over the far bloodier issues of outraged pride, jealousy and a bitter sense of rejection and injustice; of frustrated sexual urges, ambition, envy and greed. The battle between Catherine of Aragon and Anne Boleyn recognized none of the rules of war, and in the end, of course, it destroyed them both.

Two more dissimilar women than these two deadly adversaries can hardly be imagined. In 1527 Catherine was in her forty-second year. As a girl she had been pretty, small and well made, with a clear pink and white skin and quantities of russet-coloured hair, which the chronicler Edward Hall had specially noticed as being 'of a very great length, beautiful and goodly to behold'. Now her once slender figure was thickened with repeated child-bearing, and her lovely hair had darkened to a muddy brown, but visiting ambassadors still remarked on the excellence of her complexion. A dumpy little woman with a soft, sweet voice which had never lost its trace of foreign accent, and the imperturbable dignity which comes from generations of pride of caste, she faced the enemy armoured by an utter inward conviction of right and truth, and her own unbreakable will.

Henry's partisans have accused his first wife of spiritual arrogance, of bigotry and bloody-mindedness, and undoubtedly she was one of those uncomfortable people who would literally rather die than compromise over a moral issue. There's also no doubt that she was an uncommonly proud and stubborn woman. But to have yielded would have meant admitting to the world that she had lived all her married life in incestuous adultery, that she had been no more than 'the King's harlot', the Princess her daughter worth no more than any man's casually begotten bastard; and it would have meant seeing another woman occupying her place. The meekest of wives might well have jibbed at such self-sacrifice; for one of Catherine's background and temperament it was unthinkable. But what had started as the simple defence of her marriage was soon to develop into the defence of something infinitely greater. As time

54

went by and the struggle for the divorce unfolded, the Queen began to realize that she was fighting not merely for her own and her daughter's natural rights but for her husband's soul and the souls of all his people against the forces of darkness which seemed more and more to be embodied in the seductive, dark-eyed person of Mistress Anne Boleyn.

Historians, especially nineteenth-century historians, have generally taken for granted that it was Henry's pressing need for a son and heir which impelled him to seek a divorce from his barren wife and which alone sustained him through the long and blood-stained battle with Rome, but that was not how it looked to his own contemporaries. Naturally the King wanted a son, and everyone would have felt happier if there had been a Prince of Wales and, ideally, a Duke of York too, growing up in the royal nursery. But times had changed. In the 1520s, England was settled, united and prosperous, and the wars of York and Lancaster were fading into history. There was really very little reason why Henry's daughter, suitably married, of course – perhaps to one of her Plantagenet cousins or even to her other cousin, the young King of Scotland – should not have succeeded him. At eleven years old Mary was a healthy, promising little girl who would soon be of child-bearing age herself. Why shouldn't she provide sons to carry on the royal line? The fact that her father would not even consider this commonsense solution to his problem but, on the contrary, was proposing to repudiate the one heir he did possess and whose legitimacy no one else would have questioned, argued to his more cynical subjects that it was not the King's tender conscience or his anxiety over the succession which pricked him on so much as his desire for another woman. 'The common people,' commented Edward Hall, himself a staunch King's man, 'being ignorant of the truth and in especial women and others that favoured the Queen, talked largely and said that the King would for his own pleasure have another wife.' But the plain truth, as it seemed to many of those watching the progress of events, was that Henry was quite simply besotted by a commonplace young woman, sixteen years his junior, and so obsessed with carnal lust and 'the voluptuous affection of foolish love' that high discretion and, indeed, all other considerations were banished for the time.

It's never been easy to understand just what Henry saw in Anne Boleyn, or to define the secret of her undoubted fascination – probably it lay in that mysterious quality of sexual magnetism which defies an exact definition and has very little to do with physical beauty. Certainly Anne was not beautiful in any obvious sense. A brunette with a heavy mane of glossy black hair, a sallow skin and a rather flat-chested figure, her best feature seems to have been her large dark eyes which, according to one observer, 'invited to conversation'. But she knew how to make the best of herself. She dressed well and had become a leader of fashion at Court. She was lively, sophisticated and accomplished – a charming and witty companion, well versed in the arts of pleasing. She was also intelligent and courageous, aware of her own potential and restlessly seeking fulfilment in a world which offered few opportunities to ambitious, energetic and dissatisfied young women. Less attractive traits were her vindictive, sometimes vicious temper, her bitter tongue and her long memory for a grudge.

Did Anne ever feel any spark of genuine affection for Henry? Was she the helpless victim of her own nature and environment, unable to resist the pressures being brought to bear on her? Or was she simply an adventuress, motivated by personal envy and greed? Impossible now to judge with any certainty, but having once accepted the King's proposal, her situation can perhaps be compared to that of the young lady of Riga, who was so unwise as to go for a ride on a tiger – having once mounted the creature, there was no way to go but on. There is a story that Queen Catherine, who in general ignored her rival's pretensions with well-bred indifference – just as she had always ignored the existence of her husband's other passing fancies – was once playing cards with Anne and was heard to remark: 'My lady Anne, you have the good hap to stop at a king, but you are not like the others, you will have all or nothing.' Catherine herself had once waited out seven long years, just as obstinately determined to stake her future on an all-or-nothing throw. Perhaps they were not really so very unlike, these two tenacious warriors.

In July 1529 the Pope, reacting to pressure from the Emperor, at last agreed to take the King of England's matrimonial cause into his own hands, thus putting an end to Henry's hopes of getting a quick (and favourable) decision from an English Church court. This grievous disappointment was laid at Cardinal Wolsey's door, and the Cardinal's enemies, with Anne Boleyn at their head, closed in for the kill. According to George Cavendish, the estrangement between Wolsey and the King was 'the special labour of Mistress Anne', who had neither forgotten nor forgiven the Cardinal's part in blighting her romance with young Percy, and by the autumn the new Imperial envoy in London was reporting that the great minister's downfall seemed complete.

Mistress Anne now went everywhere with the King. She had her own apartments at Court and was able to indulge her taste in dress to the full, as well as enjoying the flattery and attentions normally bestowed on a royal favourite. In December further honours were showered on the Boleyn family. Sir Thomas became Earl of Wiltshire and Ormonde; Anne's brother George received the title of Viscount Rochford, while she herself was in future to be known as the Lady Anne Rochford. At a state banquet held to mark the occasion, Anne took precedence over all the ladies present (who did not include Queen Catherine) and was given the place of honour at the King's side. 'The very place allotted to a crowned Queen', wrote the Emperor's ambassador indignantly. 'After dinner', continued Messire Eustace Chapuys, 'there was dancing and carousing, so that it seemed as if nothing were wanting but the priest to give away the nuptial ring and pronounce the blessing.'

But appearances were deceptive, and after nearly two years the ultimate prize was, in fact, as far away as ever. The King might talk of proceeding by his own authority, but this was not as simple as it sounded, and Parliament showed an obstinate reluctance to assist him. Indeed, apart from Henry, the Lady

Anne and the pushful, unscrupulous clique which had attached itself to the Boleyns, nobody liked the idea of the divorce, and sympathy for the Queen was strong among all classes of Englishmen and their wives – especially their wives. The women of England could see in Catherine's present predicament an implied threat to every respectable wife and mother. After all, if the King could today cast off his virtuous and faithful consort in order to take another, younger wife, who could tell what his subjects might be able to do tomorrow? For the vast majority of women the sanctity of the marriage bond was their only security against a harsh and hostile world, and the sight of bold, black-eyed Anne Boleyn flaunting herself, bejewelled and triumphant, at the King's right hand caused much bitter and deeply-felt resentment.

While the Pope continued to delay, apparently hoping that if he waited long enough the problem might go away of its own accord, Catherine begged and implored him to take a firm stand, to settle the case without more ado and deliver her from the pains and torments to which she was daily being exposed. Like many another deserted wife, the Queen could not bring herself to face the fact that her husband had changed, that he was deliberately rejecting her of his own free will. No, it was just that he had fallen into the clutches of a wicked woman who had bewitched him and evil counsellors who were leading him astray. These people were the real enemy, and if the Holy Father would only stop their tongues and take away their hope of making mischief by proceeding swiftly to judgement, Henry would soon become his normal sweet self again. 'I trust so much in the natural goodness and virtue of the King, my lord,' wrote Catherine pathetically, 'that if I could only have him with me two months as he used to be, I alone should be powerful enough to make him forget the past.'

But by the time this letter was written, Henry had already seen, or been shown, an ingenious solution to his marital problems. Parliament might not be prepared to help him directly to get his divorce, but there would be no difficulty in persuading the Commons to attack the Church. What Henry needed was the submission of his own clergy – with that he could proceed independently of the Pope, while still preserving at least the appearances of law and orthodoxy. In order to obtain that submission, what better weapon could he use than the long-standing, smouldering anti-clericalism of the bourgeois laity? And so, indeed, it proved. By the spring of 1532 the King had assumed supreme religious power in his own realm, and the English clergy had been terrorized into surrendering all their ancient, jealously-guarded freedom from secular control.

This revolution, for such it was, had been master-minded by Thomas Cromwell, the King's new counsellor and hatchet-man, and now only one obstacle remained. William Warham, Archbishop of Canterbury, was an old man, ailing and frightened, but there was a point beyond which he could not be driven. He would not disobey the Pope's ban on any hearing of the divorce case in England. Then, in August, Providence came to the King's aid, and death removed the Archbishop from his path.

On the morning of Sunday, 1 September, an extraordinary scene was enacted in the presence chamber at Windsor Castle. Escorted by the officers of arms and flanked by two countesses, the Lady Anne Rochford, wearing a narrow-sleeved gown of crimson velvet, her hair hanging loose about her shoulders, knelt before the King, while Stephen Gardiner, Bishop of Winchester, read aloud the letters patent creating her Marquess of Pembroke – an important peer in her own right. Henry then invested his sweetheart with the panoply of her new rank and presented her with another document, granting her an independent income of a thousand pounds a year. It was an unusual, even an unprecedented occasion, but the assembled audience, which included the French ambassador and the dukes of Norfolk and Suffolk, did not fail to notice a significant omission in the wording of the new marquess's patent of creation. The title and the income would pass to the heirs male of her body, but the standard qualifying phrase 'lawfully begotten' had not been included. By agreeing to, or, more likely, insisting on, that omission, the Lady Anne was making what amounted to a public announcement that she had at last become the King's mistress in the obvious sense of the word. She was ninety-nine per cent certain now of final victory, but just in case anything should go wrong at the last moment, she was taking steps to insure her future and that of any child she might bear.

Anne had played an active part throughout the struggle for the divorce – cultivating anyone she thought might be helpful (especially the French, who could be relied on to put a spoke in the Spanish-Imperialist wheel whenever possible) and building a party for herself among the progressive anti-papalist element at home – but by far her most potent weapon had always been her own sexual attractions and her prudent refusal to allow Henry to proceed to the 'ultimate conjunction'. This in itself was no small achievement. To the world at large the sight of a young woman living unprotected in the King's household, his constant companion and often occupying adjoining apartments, naturally meant only one thing. But when the King on various occasions informed various sceptical audiences that the Lady Anne was living under his roof in perfect virtue, the overwhelming probability is that he was speaking the truth. Unsatisfied desire would certainly appear to offer the most likely and logical explanation for Anne's undiminished influence and Henry's anxious, almost slavish devotion.

By surrendering to her lover before the knot was actually tied, Anne was taking a calculated risk. She had made many enemies during the past five years, and her position depended entirely on the King's continuing ardour. If his long-anticipated gratification proved an anti-climax, if she failed to hold him during the months which must still pass before a new and pliant Archbishop could be enthroned at Canterbury, then she would have played her last card. But Anne Boleyn had never lacked self-confidence, and she was gambling now on conceiving quickly, an event which would, she reckoned, put an end to delay. The gamble paid off. By the middle of January 1533 she was able to tell the King that she was pregnant, and on the twenty-fifth of the month she and Henry were married – or perhaps it would be more accurate to say that they went through a form of marriage, since, in spite of everything, the King was still legally tied to his first wife. The ceremony was performed in one of the turret rooms at Whitehall 'very early in the morning before day' and so secretly that the identity of the priest and witnesses remains uncertain. Henry would probably have preferred to wait until Thomas Cranmer, Archbishop-elect of Canterbury, could give him his 'divorce' in proper form – it would have looked better that way – but Anne's pregnancy had altered everything, and no matter what corners had to be cut, her child must be born in wedlock.

For Anne herself that scrambling, furtive marriage in the January dawn can scarcely have had any resemblance to the royal wedding, the triumph she had once envisaged. In normal circumstances a wedding was always a joyous occasion and one to be celebrated as publicly as possible by family and friends. Secret or clandestine marriages – that is, those without previous publication of the banns on three separate Sundays or holy days – were frowned on by the Church and by society in general. A secret contract or handfasting between two impetuous young people might well frustrate the carefully laid plans of their elders and could lead to bitter ill-feeling among neighbours, especially when land or property was involved. The Church also remembered that in the case of a secret marriage, perhaps irregularly conducted and without proper safeguards, it was the woman who would be most likely to suffer and possibly be led into mortal sin.

The Tudors took the whole business of marriage – a solemn contract entered into for life and sanctified by the Church – with great seriousness. It was universally accepted that a father's first duty to his daughter was to provide her with the best and most suitable husband available, and many child betrothals or spousals were arranged as an insurance against a hazardous future. This initial form of contract, known as *de futuro*, as the promises were made in the future tense, was not a binding one. It was, in fact, little more than a conditional statement of intent to arrange a marriage at some future date. If, later on, the situation had changed, some impediment had been discovered, or the young people concerned objected, then the agreement could be terminated by mutual consent – unless, of course, there had been cohabitation. If all went well, the next stage was the *de praesenti* betrothal with the vows exchanged in the present tense. By this time the financial arrangements would have been completed, the dowry and marriage settlements agreed on, and, if the bride was an heiress, prudent relatives would have seen to it that her property was secured to herself and her children.

The betrothal *per verba de praesenti* could be celebrated at a public and formal ceremony, it could take place quietly at home, or it could simply be a man and a woman promising to marry one another in the presence of a couple of witnesses. Whatever the circumstances, it was binding and indissoluble, and any attempt to marry someone else after entering into a *de praesenti* contract was illegal. Even after a marriage had been completed and blessed by the Church, it could still be invalidated and the children bastardized if evidence of a previous *de praesenti* betrothal were to be produced; hence the insistence on due care and deliberation over the preliminaries and as much publicity as possible.

The Church had always recognized the binding nature of private spousals, but it insisted on a religious ceremony to complete and sanctify the union and impress on everyone concerned the holiness of the estate of matrimony. In the vast majority of cases this ceremony took the form of a public church wedding, but it could also be a private family occasion or be as secret as the King's marriage to his Lady. It must, though, be performed by a priest and be witnessed by two or more other persons. The content and wording of the marriage service has changed very little over the centuries: the last opportunity to disclose any impediment or irregularity, confirmation of the *de futuro* promises in the 'I will' of bride and groom, the giving away of the bride, a repetition of the *de praesenti* vows, the ritual of putting the ring on the bride's finger, the joining of hands and the final, awesome pronouncement – 'those whom God hath joined together let no man put asunder'. In pre-Reforma-

tion days the service was usually followed by Mass, later replaced by a wedding sermon in which the minister discoursed
on the duties and responsibilities of the married state. It was
the husband's part to provide for his wife and children, to guard
them from danger and want, to be faithful, generous and vigil-
ant over their welfare. The wife must first and foremost be a
good home-maker, chaste, submissive and, God willing, fruitful; for no one ever forgot that marriage had been primarily
ordained for the procreation of children and their bringing-up
in a stable, God-fearing environment. The partnership aspect
of marriage, too, was always stressed. Husband and wife must
trust one another and be tolerant of each other's little failings.
They would be together now till God did them part, and it
was up to them to make the relationship a happy and successful
one.

After all this, everyone was ready for the festive part of the
proceedings, and the rest of the day (and very often several suc-
ceeding days) was given up to merrymaking, the bridal procession making its way through the streets escorted by a cheerful
band of minstrels. The traditional white wedding is, in fact,
a comparatively recent innovation, dating from about the mid-
eighteenth century, and a Tudor bride just wore her best dress
– though she usually appeared 'in her hair', that is with her
hair hanging loose over her shoulders as a symbol of virginity,
and garlanded with flowers. Everyone else was in their best
clothes, and the home had been swept and garnished for the
occasion. There was music for dancing and food and drink in
as great an abundance as possible – if money was short, friends
and neighbours would rally round to supply the deficiencies
– and then, as now, the young couple would be showered with
gifts of plate and linen and other such useful objects to help
them set up house. But there was no 'going away', no honey-
moon and precious little privacy, for the culmination of the
jollity of every wedding day was the public bedding of bride
and groom.

It was the bridesmaids' duty to prepare the bride for bed,
to throw her stocking and distribute her garters and the knots

of ribbon from her gown (if these favours had not already been snatched off her in the general horseplay), before the groom arrived, surrounded by his friends. At grand weddings there would probably be a bishop or two on hand to bless the bridal bed, but in every case everybody who could still stand up expected to come crowding into the nuptial chamber to offer good wishes, encouragement and all too explicit advice. What sort of an ordeal this must have been for a shy girl or a nervous, inexperienced young man one can only speculate, but it was the same for everybody – an inescapable initiation ceremony. (In the royal divorce case, much play had been made over the long-ago bedding of Catherine of Aragon and Prince Arthur, someone helpfully remembering how in the morning Arthur had called for a drink, saying he had been in Spain that night and found it thirsty work.) The newly-weds would get a few hours alone together, and then the minstrels would strike up a merry tune under their window and the family would come surging back, bearing refreshments and full of anxious enquiries as to how things had gone.

Anne Boleyn might have missed all the merry sport, the excitement and the triumph normally enjoyed by a bride on her wedding day, but there would be other, less ephemeral triumphs to come; the child now growing in her womb would ensure that, and she was content at last to relax a little and await developments. These following with gratifying speed. In March Thomas Cranmer was consecrated Archbishop of Canterbury, and within a fortnight had written to the King begging permission to investigate his 'great cause of matrimony'. No one was in doubt as to the outcome of such an investigation, but even before it could begin, Anne, 'loaded with diamonds and dressed in a gorgeous suit of gold tissue', had appeared at Easter Mass in royal state, the trumpets sounding before her and the Duke of Norfolk's daughter carrying her train.

Meanwhile, Queen Catherine, exiled from the Court, not allowed to see or communicate with her daughter, humiliated, forsaken and, to all intents and purposes, defeated, had by no means given up the struggle. The previous autumn she had tried, yet again, to warn her nephew the Emperor of the grave dangers facing the Catholic faith if her case, which she now saw clearly was no longer hers alone, were not settled as a matter of urgency; and, she added, 'what passes here every day is so ugly and against God and touches the honour of the King my lord so nearly, that I cannot bear to write it'.

Eustace Chapuys, the imperial ambassador and Catherine's firm friend and champion, was of the opinion that although Henry might be by nature kind and generously inclined, his association with Anne had so perverted him that he scarcely seemed the same man, and during the momentous spring of 1533 Catherine was presented with fresh evidence of just how much her husband had changed. In April she received a deputation headed by the dukes of Norfolk and Suffolk, who descended on the remote Bedfordshire manor where she was now living. She was to renounce her title of Queen and would in future be regarded simply as Arthur's widow, with the rank of Princess Dowager. Unless she accepted the situation without further argument, her allowance would be reduced to less than a quarter of the sum she had been receiving. In any case, Norfolk told her, further resistance was useless. 'She need not trouble any more about the King, for he had taken another wife.'

Catherine was unmoved, at least outwardly. As long as she lived, she answered, she would entitle herself Queen as was her right as Henry's lawful wife. As far as her housekeeping expenses were concerned, she was at her husband's mercy. She hoped he would continue to allow her enough for herself, her confessor, a physician and two maids for her chamber. If even that was too much to ask, then she would willingly go about the world begging alms for the love of God.

With Henry's emissaries Catherine maintained her brave and dignified façade, but to Eustace Chapuys she wrote bitterly, 'there is no justice for me or my daughter'. Chapuys entirely agreed with her and told his master he was afraid 'that the moment this accursed Anne sets her foot firmly in the stirrup, she will try to do the Queen all the harm she possibly can and the Princess Mary also, which is the thing your aunt dreads most'. Chapuys reported that anger and resentment over the Queen's ill-treatment was now so widespread that very little outside encouragement would be needed to make the English people rise up and force the King to put away his concubine; and he added bluntly that, considering the insults being offered to a lady of his House, he thought the Emperor could scarcely avoid making some warlike gesture.

At the end of May, Thomas Cranmer obediently pronounced the King's first marriage to have been null and void from the beginning and his second good and valid. Three days later Anne was crowned with all customary pomp. The streets of London were hung with banners, in Cheapside a conduit ran with white wine and claret, and the usual pageants and tableaux had been staged along the processional route from the Tower to Westminster. The King's Lady had got her public triumph at last, but although the citizens came out to enjoy the show and the free drink, they remained obstinately un-impressed by the sight of their new Queen in her gleaming white gown and necklace of pearls 'as big as chick peas'. To them she would always be that 'goggle-eyed whore Nan Bullen', the cause of all good Queen Catherine's sufferings.

But there was no popular uprising, no armed intervention from abroad. The Emperor, with the cares of half Europe on his shoulders, was understandably reluctant to add war with England to his problems, and, in any case, Catherine herself vetoed the idea. She would not burden her conscience with the sin of rebellion against her husband, nor could she bring herself to involve innocent men and women in her troubles. She might have brought little good to the English people, she said sadly, but she would never deliberately bring them harm.

For the three years of life which were left to her, torn with anxiety for her daughter, heartsick at England's descent into heresy and schism, and in the face of an unremitting campaign of mean and spiteful persecution, Catherine fought on alone. Not for a thousand deaths, not for any consideration in the world, would the daughter of the Catholic Kings of Spain consent to blacken her honour or endanger her immortal soul. Many years later Eustace Chapuys was to remember her as the most virtuous woman he had ever known and the highest-hearted, 'but too quick to trust that others were like herself, and too slow to do a little ill that much good might come of it'. Thomas Cromwell, to whom Catherine's obstinacy and powerful foreign connections represented a tiresome and possibly dangerous obstacle in the way of his plans for creating an all-powerful secular state, told Chapuys that Nature had wronged the Queen in not making her a man, as but for her sex, 'she might have surpassed all the heroes of history'. As for Henry, he had long since had to resign himself to the fact that he would never win an argument with his first wife and had therefore wisely confined himself to bullying her through intermediaries. But, like Cromwell, he was in no doubt of her heroic qualities. 'The Lady Catherine', he is reported to have said, 'is a proud, stubborn woman of very high courage. Had she taken it into her head to act, she could easily have mustered an army and waged war against me as fiercely as ever her mother did in Spain.'

In March 1534 the Pope in full consistory at last proceeded to judgement in the matter of the King of England's divorce, pronouncing the marriage of Henry and Catherine to be good and valid in the eyes of God and the Church. He was four years too late, for Catherine, for her daughter and for the Catholic Church in England.

Perhaps no other episode in our history raises so many and such far-reaching 'ifs' as does the Divorce. It was an age when the domestic accidents of a handful of families could and did affect the fate of nations, and if any one of Catherine's boy babies had lived, it seems pretty safe to say that the world would never have heard of Anne Boleyn. If Catherine had been a different type of woman, content to take the easy way out, then it is equally safe to say that there would have been no breach with Rome in the early 1530s. To say that if Henry had not become infatuated with Anne, in her own way just as strong-willed and courageous a woman as her rival, there would have

CHAPTER FOUR

Bound to
Obey and Serve

Anne Boleyn's child was born at Greenwich Palace, between three and four o'clock on the afternoon of Sunday, 7 September, and it was a girl – a black disappointment, naturally, for both parents. Still, there was nothing to be done but put a good face on it and hope for better luck next time. A solemn Te Deum for the Queen's safe delivery was sung in St Paul's Cathedral, and on the following Wednesday the baby was christened with all due ceremony at the Friars' Church in Greenwich and given the name Elizabeth, in honour of the King's long-dead mother. Henry's next step was to deprive his elder daughter of her royal title – in future she would be known merely as the Lady Mary, the King's daughter – while her little half-sister became the new Princess of England. At the end of March 1534, Parliament finally ratified the Boleyn marriage, settling the succession on Anne's children and making it a treasonable offence to question the validity of the royal divorce and re-marriage by deed, word or writing.

It was unfortunate that Anne should have miscarried just about the time the Act of Succession was passing into law and again probably early in June. In July she was announced to be pregnant once more, but this time her hopes proved false, and by September she had been obliged to confess her mistake. It was beginning to look as if the King's second wife was going to be as unfortunate as his first, and for Anne that summer brought the beginnings of fear. Already Henry's eye was starting to wander, and even before the birth of Elizabeth there had been a vicious little quarrel caused by his amorous advances to some unnamed lady. Anne, it seems, had reproached him, making use of 'certain words' which caught Henry on the raw, and had been told in return 'that she must shut her eyes and endure as those who were better than herself had done, and that she ought to know that he could at any time lower her as much as he had raised her'. During the summer of 1534 there was more trouble over the King's marked attentions to 'a very handsome young lady of this Court'. When Anne, in a rage, attempted to get rid of the girl, Henry intervened, telling her that 'she ought to be satisfied with what he had done for her; for, were he to begin again, he would certainly not do as much; she ought to consider where she came from, and many other things of the same kind'.

These and other scraps of gossip, lovingly collected and relayed by Eustace Chapuys, might not amount to very much in themselves, but they made it clear that the King's white-hot physical passion had now largely burned itself out, and that without it there was precious little in the way of mutual respect or shared interests to hold the couple together. It was also becoming painfully clear that Anne's bitter tongue and habit of making scenes were doing nothing to improve matters.

The root of the trouble, of course, lay in her terrifying failure to produce a son. If only she had been able to justify herself by presenting Henry with the longed-for male heir, she would probably have felt secure enough to ignore his various fancy ladies with the fortitude expected of wives in her position. Husbandly infidelity was something which most women had to put up with at some time or other; for although married men were regularly enjoined by moralists to be faithful, in practice public opinion took a tolerant view of lapses – especially in the upper reaches of society – and wives who complained too loudly got little sympathy.

A contributory cause of Anne's disquiet lay in the intransigent attitude of the rival heiress. Mary, now eighteen, was refusing as stubbornly as her mother to accept relegation. Although she had been separated from her friends and was currently being forced to live as a virtual prisoner in the nursery establishment set up for Elizabeth and ruled by Anne's relations, there was so far no sign that loneliness, insult and neglect were doing anything to break her spirit. Anne knew very well that the great majority of the English people still regarded Mary as the rightful heir and would go on doing so in spite of fifty Acts of Parliament. She also knew that as long as Mary maintained her resistance, declaring herself to be the King's 'lawful daughter born in true matrimony', she would represent a serious threat to Elizabeth's prospects.

The battle of the mothers and daughters continued with undiminished bitterness throughout 1534 and 1535, but in the face of the old Queen's terrible, implacable patience and Mary's gallant young defence of her birthright, it often seemed as though Anne could only rage in furious impotence. She might cry shrilly that both Catherine and Mary deserved death for their disobedience but, despite Eustace Chapuys's fluently expressed fears on the subject, there was no real indication that the King intended to take up the suggestion.

The summer of 1535 saw the executions of John Fisher, once Margaret Beaufort's friend and confidant, and Thomas More, once the close friend of both Henry and Catherine, for their obstinate refusal to accept Henry Tudor's competence to act as their supreme earthly authority on matters spiritual. Since Catherine and Mary also refused to accept the royal supremacy, this should logically have led to their deaths as well. But it was one thing to kill subjects – even subjects of the calibre and international reputation of More and Fisher – it was something else again to kill your own ex-wife and daughter. In any case, Catherine was ageing now; her next birthday would be her fiftieth and her health, not surprisingly, was poor – her long fight must surely soon be ended, and if she died in her bed, there would be no risk of unpleasant repercussions from abroad. As for Mary, she could sooner or later be brought to heel, and she would probably be more amenable to pressure once her mother's example was gone. So, at least, Henry seems to have reasoned, but Anne was not appeased, and her hatred of Catherine and Catherine's daughter was becoming an obsession. It might be beyond her power to hurt Catherine more than she had already done, but Mary was still within reach, and it was on Mary that she vented the hysterical spite – product of her own desperate sense of insecurity – which had already made her so many unnecessary enemies. For her part Mary loathed her stepmother and all she stood for with a deadly corrosive bitterness that was to poison her whole life.

In the autumn of 1535 the pattern of the King's domestic affairs began to change. In October Anne accompanied him on a tour of Hampshire, where, it was reported, they were merry together and out hawking every day. In November Anne was definitely pregnant again, but Henry's brief resurgence of passion soon passed, and he was now paying open court to one of his wife's maids of honour. Mistress Jane Seymour was a quiet little blonde in her mid-twenties, undistinguished by beauty or noble birth. She was, however, a well-mannered girl, docile and undemanding – a shining contrast to Anne's shrewish, over-bearing ways. Anne, as usual, reacted violently, and according to one account, there was often 'much scratching and by-blows between the Queen and her maid'.

Then, early in January 1536, Catherine of Aragon died at last. For the past two years she had been living in almost total seclusion at Kimbolton, a gloomy, fortified manor house on the edge of the fen country. Ever since her arrival at Kimbolton Catherine had kept entirely to her own rooms, refusing to recognize the existence of those officers of the household who had been sworn to her as Princess Dowager. She still retained a handful of Spanish attendants, and her maids cooked her food before her eyes as a precaution against poison. She had been ill on and off for more than a year when, at the end of December, Eustace Chapuys received a message from Catherine's doctor telling him that, if he wanted to see her alive, he must come quickly. She was asking for him and also asking to see her daughter. Chapuys got permission to go to Kimbolton, but his request that Mary should be allowed to say goodbye to her mother was refused. Henry had no intention of risking any stiffening of her resistance which might result from some death-bed promise. Against this, considerations of compassion and ordinary humanity had no chance.

Catherine died on the afternoon of Friday, 7 January, and almost her last act had been to dictate a letter to her 'most dear lord, king and husband'. She reminded him of 'the health and safeguard' of his soul which he ought to prefer before all worldly matters, and especially before the care and pampering of his body. 'For the which', she wrote, 'you have cast me into many calamities and yourself into many troubles.' But she forgave him everything and prayed that God would do the same. 'Lastly,' she ended, 'I make this vow, that mine eyes desire you above all things' and, unconquered to the very end, she signed herself 'Catherine, the Queen'.

Henry's reaction, when he heard of the death of the woman who had loved him faithfully for more than twenty years, was one of uncomplicated relief. 'God be praised,' he exclaimed, 'now there is no fear of war.' As for Anne, she, too, rejoiced in public, but in private it was different. 'I am her death, as she is mine,' she is reputed to have said of Catherine, and as a prophecy it was to prove remarkably accurate. Anne had known for more than a year that the King would be only too glad of an excuse to be rid of her, but as long as Catherine lived, he had shrunk from the social and political complications which would have resulted from discarding yet another wife. The country had, with difficulty, contained two Queens – not even Henry could have expected it to contain three.

Anne had one hope left. She was still pregnant, and if only she could carry this child to term, if only it were a boy and healthy, she might yet come safely into harbour. Catherine of Aragon was buried in Peterborough Cathedral on 29 January and, by a particularly cruel irony of fate, on the very day of the funeral, 'Queen Anne was brought abed and delivered of a man child before her time, for she said that she had reckoned herself but fifteen weeks gone with child.' It was the final disaster. She had failed and failed again, and the King was tired of her – tired of the scenes she made, tired of her mocking laughter and her nagging tongue. Nothing, it was generally accepted, became a woman like silence, and a man tied to a shrewish, scolding wife was always an object of amused, slightly contemptuous pity. A man tied to a barren shrew could only be pitied. Most husbands so unfortunately situated had to put up with it as best they could, but the King was privileged, and his impatience to make a fresh start was becoming increasingly obvious to all interested observers. Eustace Chapuys reported that Henry scarcely spoke to his concubine these days and was telling certain close friends, in the strictest confidence of course, that he had been tricked into his second marriage by witchcraft and therefore considered it to be null and void. God clearly shared this view and was once more manifesting divine disapproval by denying him male children.

But there was to be no second royal divorce. Henry wanted no reminder of his 'great folly', and no more contumacious ex-wives to disturb his peace. Even divorced, Anne would still be Marquess of Pembroke, a personality in her own right with an independent income. Unpopular though she had always been, she was not entirely without friends and influence in certain circles, and, with her child having once been recognized as heir presumptive, she might easily become a dangerous embarrassment – especially since she was not likely to be inhibited by any of Queen Catherine's scruples when it came to stirring up political strife. A more final solution to the problem would have to be found, and at the beginning of May 1536 Anne was arrested, together with five men (including her brother George) who were accused of being her lovers, and taken to the Tower. Apart from adultery and incest, the Queen was charged with despising her marriage, entertaining malice against the King and affirming that she would never love him in her heart. She and her lovers were also accused of having conspired the King's death.

Adultery might be a moral rather than a criminal offence, but an adulterous wife could expect no mercy from a society organized on strictly patriarchal lines. Her husband would be perfectly entitled to turn her out of his house, and, if her own relations refused to take her back, her future would be nobody else's concern. Hence the constant harping by preachers and moralists of every shade of opinion on the importance of wifely chastity and the avoidance of idleness, vanity, bad company and unnecessary jaunting about the streets, where temptation might be expected to lie in wait for an inexperienced or foolish young woman. Husbands, too, were urged to be watchful and guard their wives who, as the weaker vessels, would be less able to withstand the lures of Satan.

This so-called 'double standard' of morality, which has caused so much anguish through the centuries, was not merely a matter of male pride and possessiveness. It was based on inescapable biological fact and the haunting fear that an upright citizen might be tricked into giving his name to another man's gettings or, worse, that land and property might pass to some cuckoo in the nest and a noble line be dishonoured forever. It followed, therefore, that adultery, even suspicion of adultery, committed by a King's wife, was tantamount to treason. To cast doubt on the purity of the royal line, on which the peace and welfare of the whole country depended, was the ultimate crime. No one disputed that. Whether or not Anne Boleyn was guilty as charged is quite another matter, and there is every probability that she was not. On the other hand, she had certainly been indiscreet in her dealings with the young gentlemen of the Privy Chamber – indiscreet enough to give at least some semblance of credibility to an indictment listing ten separate occasions on which the Queen was said to have procured and incited the King's daily and familiar servants to violate and carnally know her.

Anne herself denied all the charges absolutely and, although she had suffered something close to a nervous breakdown when she was first arrested, she faced her judges – twenty-six peers of the realm who included her uncle, the Duke of Norfolk, and her old sweetheart Henry Percy, now Earl of Northumberland – with courage and dignity. As in the case of most political trials, the proceedings were little more than a formality and the actual guilt or innocence of the accused an irrelevance. Anne's real crime was her failure to produce a son, compounded by the fact that she'd been the cause of the King's making a lovesick fool of himself before the world. Anne knew this as well as anyone, but she heard with composure the sentence of burning or beheading at the King's pleasure. She was ready for death, she said calmly, and only regretted that the other prisoners, all innocent and loyal subjects of the Crown, had to die for her sake.

Henry's revenge seemed complete, but it appeared that he was not content with killing the woman he had once sworn to love 'unchangeably' – he meant to annul their marriage as well. Ostensibly the reason was to bastardize Anne's daughter (for one so set on establishing the succession, the King was prodigal in disposing of heirs), but was he also perhaps eager to expunge all traces of a thoroughly unsatisfactory and slightly discreditable interlude, to wipe the slate clean and to forget?

In order to provide grounds for an annulment, Thomas Cromwell tried to establish the existence of a pre-contract between Anne and Henry Percy, but Northumberland denied this so furiously and so categorically that the Secretary was forced to fall back on the King's own misconduct with Anne's elder sister. This was unfortunate because it drew attention to an inconvenient fact, always hitherto carefully ignored. Canon law made no distinction between a legal and an illicit connection, and Henry's intercourse with Mary Boleyn made Anne just as much his sister-in-law as ever Catherine of Aragon had been. On 17 May Thomas Cranmer obediently provided a decree of nullity, and that other inconvenient fact – that Anne had been condemned for adultery having never been a wife – was also brushed aside.

This would be the first time an English queen consort had suffered death by judicial execution, and there was considerable public interest in the event. There had also been a significant shift of public opinion in Anne's favour. Not that many people felt much sympathy for her personally, but, remarked Chapuys, 'there are some who murmur at the mode of procedure against her and speak variously of the King'. Thomas Cromwell had stage-managed the Queen's downfall with his usual efficiency and had no desire to see the final scene marred by any anti-government demonstrations. He was particularly anxious that no adverse reports should be carried overseas and gave strict orders that all foreigners were to be excluded from the precincts of the Tower. This may have been the reason for a sudden, last-minute postponement of the execution date, which had been set for 18 May. Anne chafed at the delay and complained to William Kingston, Lieutenant of the Tower, 'I thought to be dead by this time and past my pain.' When Kingston tried to reassure her, telling her there should be no pain to speak of, Anne remarked that she had heard the executioner was very good, adding 'and I have a little neck'. She then put both hands round her throat, laughing with what the solemn Lieutenant could only regard as most untimely levity. He had seen many men executed and women, too, but never one like this lady who, to his own knowledge, had 'much joy and pleasure in death'.

Death came at last at eight o'clock on the morning of 19 May, when 'Anne Boleyn, Queen, was brought to execution on the green within the Tower of London,' looking, according to one eye-witness, 'as gay as if she was not going to die'. The executioner from Calais, who had been brought over for the occasion, drew his great two-handed sword from its hiding-place under a pile of straw, and it was all over. Head and trunk were bundled into a makeshift coffin and buried that afternoon in the chapel of St Peter-ad-Vincula overlooking the execution ground.

And so she was gone, that strange, disconcerting creature who had conformed to none of the accepted rules of conduct. She was twenty-nine years old and 'had reigned as Queen three years, lacking fourteen days, from her coronation to her death'. There were no mourners at that hasty, unceremonious funeral. Only Eustace Chapuys, who had feared and hated Anne alive, was generous enough to give credit where it was due, and in a despatch dated on the day of her execution he praised her great courage and readiness to meet death. He also informed the Emperor that he'd heard from a reliable source that, both before and after receiving the sacrament, Anne had sworn, on the peril of her soul's damnation, that she had never been unfaithful to the King.

The King, who believed – or said he did – all the stories now circulating about the Queen's 'abominable and detestable crimes' and 'incontinent living', had been waiting with unconcealed impatience for the news that he was free again, and barely twenty-four hours later he and Jane Seymour were betrothed. On 30 May they were married in the chapel of York Place, and Jane was installed in the Queen's seat under the canopy of estate royal. Meanwhile, in the palaces of Hampton Court, Richmond and Greenwich, carpenters, painters and plasterers were hard at work obliterating Anne Boleyn's badges and coats of arms and the true lovers' knots with the linked initials HA (which had provoked rude cries of 'Ha! Ha!' from the Cockneys) and replacing them with the insignia of her successor. Jane had taken the motto 'Bound to Obey and Serve', a tactful choice, and Henry would have no cause to complain of this wife's violent temper and bitter, scolding tongue. Indeed, as a personality, Jane seems to have been silent and submissive almost to the point of non-existence. But although the King enjoyed parading his new-found domestic bliss, one piece of unfinished business remained, and during the summer of 1536 he turned to strike at his elder daughter in an all-out bid to obtain her surrender.

Mary herself was still clinging, as her mother had done before her, to the belief that her sufferings had been due entirely to the malign influence of Anne Boleyn, and she clearly hoped that the way would now be open for an honourable reconciliation with her father. She had yet to face the chilling truth that the change in him was permanent and that the gay, easy-going, affectionate parent she remembered from happy childhood days no longer existed.

Guided by Thomas Cromwell, who had cast himself in the role of peacemaker, Mary wrote to her father at the beginning of June, begging 'in as humble and lowly a manner as a child can' for his daily blessing, which was her chief desire in this world, and acknowledging all her past offences. 'Next unto God,' she went on, 'I do and will submit me in all things to your goodness and pleasure ... beseeching your Highness to consider that I am but a woman, and your child, who hath committed her soul only to God and her body to be ordered in this world as it shall stand in your pleasure.'

Ten days later Mary received a letter from Cromwell enclosing the draft of a formal apology which he advised her to copy and send to the King. She returned two copies of this document in which she was prostrate before the King's most noble feet, his most obedient, repentant and humble child who was ready henceforward, next to Almighty God, to put her 'state, continuance and living' in his gracious mercy. In a covering letter to the Secretary, Mary told him that, God and her conscience not offended, she had followed his advice and would continue to do so in all things concerning her duty to the King. She was grateful for his help but begged him not to press her any further, for she had now done the uttermost her conscience would suffer her.

When Cromwell had read his copy of the apology, he withheld the sealed letter for the King. There had been nothing about 'next to Almighty God' in his original, and it was a reservation which rendered Mary's submission worthless from Henry's point of view. Cromwell had staked a good deal on getting that submission, and now he wrote again, more sharply, sending yet another draft in which there was to be no 'exception'. Mary knew by this time that she was in no position to quibble over a form of words and would be lucky to escape with a general act of contrition, however abject. She returned the draft 'without adding or minishing' – just the one copy this time because she could not endure to write another.

Still it was not enough, and a commission, headed by the Duke of Norfolk, came down to the nursery palace at Hunsdon in Hertfordshire bringing with them a deposition drawn up for her signature – a deposition in which she would explicitly recognize her father as Supreme Head of the Church in England and the nullity of her mother's marriage. When Mary refused to sign, the behaviour of the commissioners finally killed any lingering hope of making peace with honour. They told her that she had so long been so obstinate towards the King's majesty that she seemed 'a monster in nature'. She was such an unnatural daughter, said one, that he doubted if she was even the King's bastard. Another added pleasantly that were she *his* daughter, he would beat her to death and knock her head against a wall until it was as soft as a boiled apple. They told her she had shown herself a traitor to the King and his laws and would be punished as such. Finally they said she could have four days to think it over and left orders that she was not to be left alone for a moment, night or day.

Nevertheless, Mary did manage to make last desperate appeals to both Chapuys and Cromwell. But Chapuys, her friend and ally, could not help her in this extremity and advised her to yield if she felt her life was really in danger. Trying to make things easier for her, he said that God looked more at the intentions than the deeds of men, and she might be better able to serve Him in the future if she gave way now. As for Cromwell, he was badly frightened. When the commission had reported their failure with Mary, Henry had flown into a calculated rage, directed not only at his daughter but at anyone else who could be suspected of sympathizing with her or encouraging her resistance. The Privy Council was in continuous session, and the King had prevailed on the judges to agree that if Mary continued to defy him, she could be proceeded against in law. According to Chapuys, Henry had been heard to swear that not only Mary should suffer for her obstinacy, but Cromwell and many others.

In his reply to her final appeal, the Secretary made it very clear that Mary could expect no further help from him. 'To be plain with you, madam,' he wrote, 'as God is my witness, I think you the most obstinate and obdurate woman that ever was.' Unless she speedily abandoned her 'evil counsels' which had brought her to the point of utter undoing, he wanted nothing more to do with her. 'For', he went on, 'I will never think you other than the most ingrate, unnatural and most obstinate person living, both to God and your most dear and benign father.' He did, however, give her one last chance, enclosing 'a certain book of articles' which she was to sign and return to him with a declaration that she thought in heart as she subscribed with hand.

When Cromwell's letter reached her, Mary knew that she was beaten. For three years she had fought bravely to defend her principles and her good name – now, utterly alone, exhausted and afraid, she gave in. At eleven o'clock one Thursday night towards the end of June, she set her name to Cromwell's book of articles, recognizing her father as the 'supreme head in earth under Christ of the Church of England' and rejecting the Bishop of Rome's 'pretended authority, power and jurisdiction within this realm'. She also acknowledged that her parents' marriage had been 'by God's law and man's law, incestuous and unlawful'.

Her reward, a few weeks later, was a visit from the King and Queen. Her stepmother gave her a diamond ring, and her father put a cheque for a thousand crowns into her hand. Chapuys reported that it was impossible to describe the King's kind behaviour towards his daughter. 'There was nothing but conversing with the Princess in private; and with such love and affection and such brilliant promises for the future, that no father could have behaved better.'

Henry was obviously immensely relieved that his terror tactics had paid off, for it had become increasingly important to secure Mary's submission in view of the growing signs of unrest among those who disliked his revolutionary policies. Already that summer the smaller monasteries were being suppressed and their revenues appropriated by the Crown, which, as at least one observer noted, was the cause of 'great lamentation by the poor people'. Mary had always been a popular figure, and she represented the old, familiar ways. She had many friends and sympathizers, too, among the older, more conservative nobility and gentry and, as long as she continued to resist, might very well have been used as a figurehead by those who sought a way of forcing the King back into the paths of righteousness.

On the more domestic level, it looked bad for the King's own daughter to be defying him. In a society based on the family unit ruled by the benevolent despotism of husband and father, filial obedience was an essential ingredient of peace and stability. It was, therefore, a virtue highly prized by parents, who were generally considered within their rights to enforce it, where necessary, however brutally. The King, as father of the national family, could least afford the continuing spectacle of dissension within his household.

Mary, brought up to revere both her parents, had undoubtedly been made to feel acutely guilty and unhappy over her difference with her father, but now she bore an even heavier burden of guilt. She begged Chapuys to ask the Pope to give her a secret absolution for what she had done, but nothing could alter the fact that she had knowingly betrayed the two things which meant most in the world to her – her religious faith and her mother's memory. The consciousness of that betrayal, made by a frightened girl of twenty, was to haunt her for the rest of her life.

Meanwhile, the King's younger daughter was being disinherited in her turn. Parliament met that June and passed a second Act of Succession, ratifying the annulment of the Boleyn marriage and settling the crown, this time, on Jane Seymour's children. At not quite three years old, this sudden diminution of her social status did not greatly concern Elizabeth, but it prompted a worried letter from Lady Bryan, the Lady Mistress of the nursery, to Thomas Cromwell. 'Now as my Lady Elizabeth is put from that degree she was in,' wrote Margaret Bryan distractedly, 'and what degree she is at now I know not but by hearsay, I know not how to order her or myself, or her women or grooms.' The child was growing fast and her wardrobe urgently needed replenishing, but where was Lady Bryan to turn for instructions and supplies? There was trouble, too, within the household. Sir John Shelton, the steward or governor, wanted Elizabeth 'to dine and sup every day at the board of estate', probably to bolster his own importance, but the Lady Mistress considered this most unsuitable. 'It is not meet for a child of her age to keep such rule yet. If she do, I dare not take it upon me to keep her Grace in health; for there she shall see divers meats, and fruits, and wine, which it would be hard for me to restrain her Grace from.' Elizabeth was already in some danger of becoming spoiled, for 'my lady hath great pain with her great teeth, and they come very slowly forth, which causeth me to suffer her Grace to have her will more than I would'. However, Lady Bryan means to put this right as soon as she can. 'I trust to God, and her teeth were well graft, to have her Grace after another fashion than she is yet, so as I trust the King's Grace shall have great comfort in her Grace. For she is as toward a child and as gentle of conditions as ever I knew any in my life, Jesu preserve her Grace.'

Thomas Cromwell added the voluble Lady Bryan's problems to his innumerable other preoccupations, and once the confusion created by the recent upheavals in the royal circle had settled down, both Mary and Elizabeth were suitably provided for. The sisters continued for the most part to share an establishment, and although they now stood on equal terms socially, Mary, as the elder, had regained a natural precedence. Many of her old friends and servants were being allowed to rejoin her, and in August Chapuys was able to report that her position was improving every day. 'Never did she enjoy so much liberty as she does now,' he wrote, 'nor was she ever served with such solemnity and honour as she is at present.' Mary was at Court that autumn, where she came first after the Queen, presenting the napkin at the meal-time ceremony after the King and Queen had washed, and taking her place at table opposite them and only a little lower down the board. Jane Seymour had once served Queen Catherine as maid of honour, and now it was noticed that she went out of her way to show consideration to Catherine's daughter, often taking her by the hand so that they could pass through a doorway side by side.

Henry still seemed satisfied by his third marriage – at least there are no stories of his unfaithfulness to this wife – but the year ended with no sign of Jane's becoming pregnant. It wasn't until March 1537 that a hopeful announcement could at last be made. On Trinity Sunday, 'like one given of God', the child quickened in its mother's womb, and Te Deums were sung in many churches, while loyal subjects everywhere prayed for a prince. Henry fussed anxiously round his wife, sending here and there for fat quails, for which she apparently had a pregnant woman's craving, and generally behaving like a model husband. He had intended to go north that summer, but in view of the Queen's condition, he cancelled all his arrangements. Jane had everything she could reasonably want, but Henry was taking no chances: 'considering that, being but a woman, upon some sudden and displeasant rumours and bruits that might by foolish or light persons be blown abroad in our absence, being specially so far from her, she might take to her stomach such impressions as might engender no little danger or displeasure to the infant'. So, to avoid such perils, the King let it be known that he would travel no further than sixty miles from the palace until the Queen had been delivered.

Hampton Court, the handsome riverside mansion built by Cardinal Wolsey in the days of his glory, had been chosen for the lying-in, and there, on 16 September, the Queen 'took her chamber' with all due ceremony; but she did not enjoy the 'good hour' so earnestly prayed for on these occasions. She went into labour during the afternoon of 9 October, and her ordeal lasted three days and two nights. At two o'clock in the morning of 12 October the child was born. It was a boy, normal and healthy. The whole country went hysterical with joy, while, at Hampton Court, preparations began at once for a christening which would be worthy of Henry Tudor's son. But in all the flurry of correspondence, the triumphant announcements carried by royal messenger to every corner of the kingdom and the letters of congratulation and thankfulness pouring into the palace, there was scarcely a mention of the woman who had at last given England a prince. This complete lack of sentimentality or even sympathy was typical of the general attitude towards childbirth. It was also the obverse side of all the splendour and ceremonial, the elaborate deference paid to the Queen. Jane, like any farmer's wife, had done her business, the business she'd been created for. She'd done it successfully and been lucky enough to survive, and really there was no more to be said.

The christening of Prince Edward took place on the fifteenth and the Queen, wrapped in velvet and fur, was carried from her bed to lie propped up with pillows on an elaborate state pallet, or sofa, to receive the guests. The ceremony lasted nearly six hours, but protocol did not release Jane until the procession had returned from the chapel and the precious baby, borne in the arms of the Marchioness of Exeter, had been presented for his parents' blessing. Three days later, the Queen collapsed in a high fever, and early on the morning of the nineteenth she received the last sacrament. She rallied briefly and seemed to be holding her own, but by 24 October she was dead.

The generally received explanation of this unfortunate occurrence was that, by the carelessness of her attendants, she had been allowed to catch cold at the christening, and Thomas Cromwell also blamed those about her for letting her eat such unsuitable food 'as her fantasy in sickness called for'. In fact, of course, as far as it is possible to be certain, she died of puerperal sepsis, or childbed fever, caused by bacterial infection of the placental site – the large raw area on the interior of the uterus – or the lacerations of the birth canal, especially likely after a long and difficult labour.

Henry was with his wife to the end and seemed genuinely grief-stricken by her death. Jane was given a state funeral, with the Princess Mary, who had lost an influential friend, acting as chief mourner. She was buried in St George's Chapel at Windsor and was the first and, as it turned out, the only one of Henry's wives to be buried as Queen. Perhaps this was fair. She was, after all, the only one who fulfilled her side of the bargain to his satisfaction.

CHAPTER FIVE

The Frailness
of Young Women

Henry embarked on the second half of his matrimonial marathon at the end of 1539, after an intensive two-year search for a bride round the Courts of Europe. Threatened with the danger of encirclement by hostile Catholic powers, England urgently needed friends abroad, but unfortunately the King of England's reputation as a husband was not now such as to re-assure the parents of marriageable daughters. He had, after all, had one wife publicly put to death; while it was freely rumoured in certain circles that he'd disposed of Catherine of Aragon by poison and callously allowed Jane Seymour to be lost 'for lack of keeping in her childbed'. In the circumstances, it was not surprising that at least one strong-minded princess should have spurned the doubtful privilege of becoming wife number four, though there is, unhappily, no authority for the story that Christina of Milan rejected Henry's flattering proposal on the grounds that she had only one head.

Negotiations with foreign royalty were further hampered by the King's determination to inspect their daughters personally, instead of following the normal diplomatic practice of trusting to portrait-painters and the reports of ambassadors. His insensi-tive attempt to stage what amounted to a 'Miss Queen of Eng-land' contest at Calais from among a shortlist of French candi-dates provoked a stinging rebuke from King François. It was not the custom of his country, remarked that monarch coldly, to send young ladies of good family to be passed in review like horses for sale. Was this, enquired his ambassador, how the knights of the Round Table had treated their womenfolk? And Henry was, for once, reduced to silence.

The quest ended at last in the north Rhineland duchy of Cleves on the Dutch–German border with the twenty-three-year-old sister of the reigning duke – a rather curious choice in view of ambassador Nicholas Wootton's reports. Anne of Cleves had, it seemed, been strictly brought-up and spent most of her time at her needlework. She could read and write, but knew no French or Latin or indeed any language except her native German, though Wootton thought she was intelligent enough to learn English quite quickly if she put her mind to it. More seriously, she could not sing or play any instrument, for, the ambassador explained, 'they take it here in Germany for a rebuke and an occasion of lightness that great ladies should be learned or have any knowledge of music'. And he added that he 'could never hear that she is inclined to the good cheer of this country'. None of this makes Anne sound a particularly suitable bride for Henry VIII, nor, contrary to legend, does the miniature painted by Hans Holbein portray any great beauty. However, in view of the increasingly serious international situation, Henry could not afford to be too choosy. An alliance in the emerging 'third world' of non-aligned north European states would be undeniably valuable – especially at a time when France and Spain were, temporarily at least, presenting a united front. So the marriage contract was signed, and Anne of Cleves landed at the port of Deal on 27 December 1539.

The story of the King's acute and freely expressed disappointment on first seeing his betrothed is perhaps sufficiently well known, but whether poor Anne was really so very unattractive may be open to some doubt. Certainly the face which looks out of Holbein's miniature is by no means without charm, and compared with, say, the portrait of Queen Jane Seymour, her successor would seem to have little to be ashamed of. According to the French ambassador, she looked older than her years – he put her down as being about thirty, was tall of stature, pitted with the smallpox and had little beauty. No one, which seems rather odd, had apparently thought fit to mention the matter of the smallpox scars to Henry, although it was a common enough defect at the time. Marillac went on to describe her countenance as 'determined and resolute', and although he admitted there was some show of vivacity in her expression, he considered it 'insufficient to counterbalance her want of beauty'.

Anne was a sturdy, big-boned, strong-featured young woman – a common enough Germanic type – but emphatically not a type admired by the sophisticates of London and Paris, and the stiff, clumsy German fashions she arrived in appeared grotesque to English eyes. All the same, Anne was not devoid of taste and was soon ordering plain black dresses of satin and damask to show off her jewellery, which seems to have been her only major extravagance. She was clearly anxious to please and adapted readily to English ways, more than fulfilling Nicholas Wootton's estimate of her ability to learn the language. She learned to play cards, too, and in spite of not being able to sing or play an instrument, her account books show that she was fond of music and also took an interest in gardens and gardening. Her first few weeks in England must have been particularly trying, since she can scarcely have failed to realize that she was being despised, but she carried off a difficult and humiliating situation with great natural dignity and composure. Given half a chance, there is no reason to suppose that this large, homely, serene and sensible girl would not have made the King a perfectly satisfactory wife.

But Henry made no attempt to overcome his initial aversion. Lacking the courage to do the honourable thing and send Anne straight home again, he went through with the wedding, complaining piteously that 'if it were not to satisfy the world and my realm, I would not do that I must do this day for none earthly thing'. But not even to satisfy the world and his realm could he bring himself to consummate the marriage, finding nothing in his bride 'to excite and provoke any lust in him'. He did, however, share her bed for a few nights, and the English matrons of the Queen's bedchamber questioned her hopefully about her condition. But when Anne told them that, when the

Margaret Beaufort: 'My lady the King's Mother'

Elizabeth of York by an unknown artist

Margaret Tudor, Queen of Scotland, c. 1520; an unauthenticated portrait attributed to Jean Perréal

Mary Tudor, Queen of France, a drawing by Clouet

LA ROYNE MARIE

Catherine of Aragon in middle-age; portrait by an unknown artist

Anne Boleyn

Jane Seymour, the mother of the heir; a portrait by Holbein

Anne of Cleves, the rejected wife; painted by Holbein

Katherine Howard

Katherine Parr attributed to William Scrots

The Lady Mary after Queen.

Queen Mary Tudor
as a young girl,
sketched by Holbein

Lady Jane Grey, an unauthenticated portrait

Queen Elizabeth I

Mary Queen of Scots
by an unknown artist

Frances Grey, Duchess of Suffolk with her second husband Adrian Stokes in 1559,
painted by Hans Eworth

The Countess of Shrewsbury, the
formidable Bess of Hardwick

The bluestocking Mildred Cooke, who
became William Cecil's second wife

King came to bed, 'he kisses me and taketh me by the hand and biddeth me "Goodnight, sweetheart"; and in the morning kisses me and biddeth me "Farewell, darling",' Lady Rochford burst out: 'Madam, there must be more than this, or it will be long ere we have a Duke of York.' 'Nay,' said Anne innocently, 'is not this enough? I am contented with this, for I know no more.'

No one, of course, supposed for a moment that the King would put up with the unsatisfactory state of his marital affairs for long, and the only question in most people's minds was how soon it would be before he took steps to extricate himself. The presence of a queen, after a two-year gap, had brought the girls to Court again and, although Anne's household was somewhat smaller than most of her predecessors' had been, there was the usual vigorous scrambling for places. Mistress Anne Basset, already established as a maid of honour, was urged by her ambitious mama to recommend her sister Katherine for a post among the Queen's maids and sent a jar of her mother's special quince preserve to offer the King as a sweetener. His Highness was graciously pleased to accept the gift and 'liked it wondrous well', but he was evidently not in any very approachable mood. Anne Basset summoned up the courage to speak for her sister, but she hesitated to press the matter or to mention certain other favours requested by her parents (there was no point in having a daughter at Court and not making use of her to further the family's interests), 'for fear how his Grace would take it'.

Katherine Basset evidently had to resign herself to staying where she was, in the service of the Countess of Rutland; but among the successful candidates for preferment with more influential relatives to pull strings on her behalf was the Duke of Norfolk's niece, young Katherine Howard, a vivacious, ripely attractive teenager. By Easter it was public knowledge that the King's volatile fancy had once more been captured, and the stage was set for a palace revolution led by the formidable Howard clan.

The disposal of Anne of Cleves proved unexpectedly painless.

The fact that she had once been tentatively betrothed to the Duke of Lorraine's son offered a convenient toehold for Henry's conscience, and by midsummer enough legal confusion had been created over the exact nature of this pre-contract to provide grounds for divorce. On 9 July Convocation unanimously pronounced the King's fourth marriage to be null and void, and four days later an obedient Parliament ratified the judgement of the clergy. The Supreme Head of the Church could reasonably expect the co-operation of his own bishops, but two additional factors had helped to smooth his path: one being that the fragile truce between the two great European power blocs was already breaking up, thus relieving England's isolation and making the German alliance expendable; while the other was the helpful attitude adopted by the Queen.

Henry had sent Anne down to Richmond in the middle of June, 'purposing it to be more for her health, open air and pleasure', though he himself remained to seek his pleasure in the capital, paying frequent visits to Mistress Katherine Howard at her grandmother's house in Lambeth. The Queen would not, of course, have understood all the ramifications of the power struggle currently in progress at Court (they remain more than somewhat obscure to this day), but she was certainly alarmed by the sudden arrest of Thomas Cromwell on a charge of high treason, which took place a few days before her own banishment. Cromwell had been the chief architect of the Cleves marriage, and Anne naturally regarded him in the light of a friend and mentor. Whether she was really afraid that she might soon be joining him in the Tower is difficult to say, but in the circumstances she could hardly be blamed for feeling nervous about her future. According to one account, she fell to the ground in a dead faint when a delegation headed by the Duke of Suffolk arrived at Richmond, believing they had come to arrest her. Her visitors, however, quickly reassured her. They had, on the contrary, been instructed to offer her what Henry considered generous terms in exchange for his freedom: an income of five hundred pounds a year, the use of two royal residences, with an adequate establishment, plus the position of the King's adopted sister with precedence over every other lady in the land except the next queen and the princesses.

Anne's immediate reaction was one of transparent relief, and she accepted with so much alacrity that Henry was surprised and even a trifle disconcerted. Some protestation, a few regretful tears, would, he felt, have been more appropriate in the face of such a sacrifice, and he insisted that Anne should write home at once, explaining how honourably she was being used and how willingly she had consented to the divorce. Until this letter had been written, Henry could not be easy in his mind, since all would depend on a woman's word, which, as any sensible man knew, meant little or nothing. It was in women's nature to be changeable, and so for a woman to promise 'that she will be no woman' was a contradiction in terms and could not be relied upon.

Anne showed no sign whatever of going back on her word, but she wrote obediently to her brother, telling him that the King, whom she could not justly have as her husband, had shown himself a most kind, loving and friendly father and brother, and had so provided for her. It was her wish, she went on, that the knot of amity concluded between their two countries should remain unbroken, and she ended: 'Only I require this of you, that ye so conduct yourself as for your untowardness in this matter I fare not the worse, whereunto I trust you will have regard.' Having dissolved their marriage, Henry had, of course, no shadow of right to keep his ex-wife in England, and he was, in effect, holding her hostage for the good behaviour of her brother and the other German princes. The Duke of Cleves was naturally not at all pleased by the turn events had taken and was anxious for his sister's return, but he and his ambassador could do little in the face of her repeated assurances that she only wished to please the King her lord, that she was being well treated and wanted to stay in England. 'God willing,' she wrote, 'I purpose to lead my life in this realm.'

Anne has often been dismissed as dull and spiritless for her meek acceptance of Henry's rejection, but her situation was totally different from that of Catherine of Aragon, and in any case the alternatives open to her were strictly limited. Had she attempted to fight the case, she would inevitably have lost it. Had she insisted on going home, she would have forfeited her alimony, and having now seen something of a wider world and the pleasures it had to offer, the prospect of returning penniless to her needlework in the narrow confines of the ducal palace at Cleves offered little attraction. She had escaped from one loveless and frightening marriage and seems to have had no inclination to try again; besides which, there was no guarantee that any other European power would recognize her English divorce. On the other hand, by accepting Henry's terms and staying on in England, she would keep a measure of financial independence and social status in a country whose people and customs she clearly found congenial. Anne evidently considered that she was getting a fair bargain and, like a sensible woman, settled down to make the best of it. Indeed, she made the most of it. In September the French ambassador reported that 'Madame of Cleves has a more joyous countenance than ever. She wears a great variety of dresses and passes all her time in sports and recreations.'

Meanwhile the King had taken his fifth wife.

Katherine Howard was in her late teens at the time of her marriage, the youngest of a family of ten children and an orphan. Her father, Lord Edmund Howard, a younger brother of the Duke of Norfolk, had been something of a ne'er-do-well, and her mother, Joyce Culpeper, had died when her youngest daughter was quite a small child. Although Lord Edmund married again, most of Joyce's family were brought up by their Howard grandmother, along with a whole tribe of Howard cousins and connections. This was in accordance with the common practice of farming out one's children, but in Lord Edmund's case it no doubt also helped to ease his chronic financial distress.

The modern trend was towards smaller households, more supervision and regulation, and greater privacy for the family; but Agnes, Dowager Duchess of Norfolk, was something of a survival from an earlier, more casual age, and her establishments at Horsham in Sussex and at Lambeth were run on generously mediaeval lines. Upwards of a hundred persons (her ladyship herself could probably not have put an exact number to them) crowded under her various roofs – family, hangers-on, poor relations, children, secretaries, tutors, servants, servants' servants, servants' families and friends – all eating, sleeping, working or not working, gambling, playing, quarrelling and making love in cheerful, insanitary propinquity. Katherine Howard and her cousins shared the maids' dormitory (two or three to a bed) with the dowager's waiting gentlewomen and what might loosely be described as the upper female servants, drawn chiefly from the daughters of the neighbouring gentry who regarded the Duchess as their natural patron. This was not an unusual arrangement – a bed to oneself, let alone a bedroom to oneself, was a luxury enjoyed only by the very greatest personages – and communal living was still accepted as the norm by most people.

Katherine was about ten years old when she came under her grandmother's care, to learn obedience, good manners, some social graces and the rudiments of household management; enough, in short, to fit her for marriage to the husband who would in due course be chosen by the family – perhaps some rising man at Court whom it would be useful to attach to the Howard interest. She was taught to read and write, but the dowager had no patience with any new-fangled notions about higher education for women and, besides, Katherine was not academically inclined. A pretty child, but bird-brained and barely literate, she grew naturally into an empty-headed adolescent, one of a bevy of giggling, chattering girls who thought of precious little but clothes, young men and how to squeeze as much fun as possible out of life before they were inexorably claimed by marriage and the painful drudgery of child-bearing. The Duchess was not deliberately neglectful of her responsibilities, but she was a busy woman, not over-gifted with imagination, and saw no reason to pay special attention to her orphaned grand-daughter. The child was getting a Christian upbringing among her kinsfolk and all the education that was good for her. She was no worse off in that respect than any of her contemporaries and would have to take her chance with the rest.

Katherine took her first chance when she was fourteen or so. She may not have possessed much in the way of intellectual equipment, but she was fully aware of her own developing body and of its effect on the opposite sex – especially on one Henry Manox, who had recently come to Horsham to give the young ladies music lessons. Katherine Howard learned more from Henry Manox than how to strike graceful chords on the lute and virginals, and they were soon making assignations to meet in unfrequented corners, where Manox became familiar with the 'secret parts' of Mistress Katherine's body. The Duchess caught them at it on at least one occasion, but she didn't seem unduly disturbed, merely scolding the guilty pair and giving orders that they were never to be left alone in future. In spite of this, the romance continued for a while, the young people exchanging messages and tokens via sympathetic third parties – a traffic which, of course, soon led to rumours of an engagement between them. Manox, in fact, was growing so confident of Katherine's affection that he boasted openly that she had promised him her maidenhead, 'though it be painful to her'. This piece of indiscretion prompted a stern warning from Mary Lassells, the Duchess's chamberer, who told him plainly that he was asking for trouble. The Howards might take a tolerant view of a bit of youthful kissing and fumbling, but they would certainly not permit one of their kinswomen to tie herself up to a mere music teacher, and if Manox persisted, he would find himself undone.

But Manox's brief ascendancy was already coming to an end. The Duchess had by this time moved with her entourage to Lambeth, and her grand-daughter's horizons were widening. The old lady herself seldom went to Court, but her palatial town house was only just across the river from Westminster, easily accessible to exciting stream of visitors, and it wasn't long before Katherine had acquired another admirer. Francis Dereham was a member of the Duke of Norfolk's household and a distant connection of the Howards, a handsome, dashing young gentleman of birth and substance and altogether a more attractive proposition than poor Henry Manox, who was ruthlessly discarded. Francis Dereham's face was soon familiar at Lambeth, and he became a regular member of that privileged group of gentlemen who could be sure of a welcome in the girls' dormitory after lights out.

The door of the 'maidens' chamber' was, in theory, locked at bedtime, but in practice this did not present a very serious barrier; keys could always be stolen or someone persuaded to 'forget' to lock up. The Duchess cannot have been entirely unaware of what was going on but took the easy-going view that girls would be girls (perhaps she thought there was safety in numbers), and as long as they kept their activities within bounds and did not create the sort of scandal she would have had to take notice of, she was prepared to turn a blind eye. So the more adventurous young men continued to sneak off upstairs after the old lady had retired for the night, taking with them wine, fruit and sweetmeats 'to make good cheer' with her maids.

This sort of merry-making did not, of course, end with midnight feasts. Katherine was older now and sexually fully mature. Dereham was both more enterprising and more experienced than Henry Manox, and they naturally progressed from caresses 'in doublet and hose' to the intimacies of a naked bed. It was impossible to keep this secret from the other inmates of the dormitory – Alice Restwold, Katherine's official bed-mate, later deposed that she at least knew very well what belonged to all that puffing and blowing behind the bed-curtains. But since Katherine and Dereham were by no means the only illicit couple making use of its facilities, the dormitory continued to observe its conspiracy of silence, although some of the older ladies began to complain of being kept awake, and the more sober spirits claimed to be shocked.

Outside the doubtful privacy of the maidens' chamber, the pair made no particular effort to conceal their attachment, generally behaving as if they were engaged. It was common knowledge in the household that they were 'far in love', and quite a few people believed that Mr Dereham would have Mrs Katherine Howard. They could be seen openly kissing and cuddling, and, on one occasion, Dereham had demanded to know why he should not kiss his own wife. In the eyes of the Church they were as good as married – for even such an informal arrangement as this, when consummated with carnal knowledge, could be held to constitute a form of marriage. Dereham unquestionably wanted to get the relationship legalized and pestered Katherine about it, but she refused to commit herself. Far from being the corrupted innocent she is sometimes depicted, Katherine Howard, it must be said, seems to have possessed all the instincts of a natural tart who knew exactly what she was doing. She'd taken the precaution of acquiring some rudimentary knowledge of birth control, boasting rather optimistically that 'a woman might meddle with a man and yet conceive no child unless she would herself', and having discovered the delights of sex, saw no reason to settle for the first man who'd bedded her.

The affair drifted on for the best part of a year, and perhaps the oddest feature of it was the Duchess's continued indulgence. When she found the couple kissing in the great gallery, she enquired sharply if they thought her house was the King's Court, but she made no effort to separate them. For some reason the old lady had a particularly soft spot for Francis Dereham, but probably the truth was that she didn't take the matter very seriously. While society at large paid lip-service to the ideal of chastity, it also accepted the inevitability of a certain amount of pre-marital intercourse. Youth was naturally lusty, life was short, and there was no point in making too much fuss about something which could hardly be prevented. In some circles, among the respectable bourgeoisie and the lesser gentry for example, it was important that a girl should be a virgin when she married, but aristocrats like the Howards could afford to adopt a more permissive attitude. Unless she had made herself really notorious, very few families were going to turn down the opportunity of a match with a Howard lady. From her knowledge of her grand-daughter, the dowager could feel confident that she would forget Dereham as quickly as she had forgotten Henry Manox the moment some more exciting prospect appeared on the scene; besides, as Katherine knew as well as anyone, in her world love and marriage were two quite separate issues. The family, if they thought about it at all, simply took it for granted that when the time came to settle her future she would be ready to fulfil her obligations as befitted one of her breeding. Meanwhile, no one grudged her a few wild oats.

The time to settle Katherine's future came in the late autumn of 1539. Her appointment to one of the much-coveted posts in the new Queen's household was, of course, thanks entirely to the patronage of her uncle the Duke, and it would certainly have been impressed upon her that she was being granted a very special opportunity and would be expected to make the most of it. Katherine herself pranced cheerfully off to Court, her head full of the dazzling social life she was about to enjoy in the company of an unlimited number of handsome young gallants, but with apparently no realization whatever that she was leaving the nursery for a dangerous adult world, a world seething with intrigue and violence where no quarter was asked or given.

Except that it was larger and grander, the structure and hierarchy of the King's household was not so very different from that of the Dowager Duchess of Norfolk. There was the same overcrowding, the same mixture of squalor, confusion and luxurious discomfort; but the Court was also a jungle, the natural habitat of predators whose teeth and claws were only imperfectly concealed by the embroidered satin, the velvet and jewels, and of whom it behoved the weak, the ignorant and the inexperienced to be very wary indeed. Nevertheless, when the grandest and most dangerous predator of all 'cast his fantasy' towards the plump, dainty morsel that was Katherine Howard, her relations were overjoyed. This was just the stroke of fortune which the family needed and had perhaps been angling for. Aunts and cousins descended in flocks to give Mistress Katherine sage advice on how to behave and 'in what sort to entertain the King and how often'. His Highness was welcomed at

Lambeth with open arms and the Howards joined in chorus to commend their young kinswoman for 'her pure and honest condition'. Any lingering memories of tales about scufflings behind the bed-curtains were naturally expunged from their collective consciousness.

Henry was now forty-nine, and the muscle of his superb athlete's body was turning rapidly to fat. But although increasing age and girth had forced him to give up the violent exercise he had once revelled in, he was still a fine figure of a man, still active and energetic, and the stimulus of his new marriage seemed to have given him a new lease of life and vigour. Katherine's exuberant vitality, her gaiety and the new-minted quality of her auburn-haired prettiness enchanted the King. She was his rose without a thorn, a jewel of womanhood, and nothing was too good for her. New dresses, expensive furs and jewellery, valuable grants of land, manors and lordships, poured forth in an apparently inexhaustible stream, while life at Court had once more become a continuous round of dancing and feasting. Katherine was still probably no more than eighteen or nineteen when she was 'showed openly as Queen' at Hampton Court on 8 August 1540. The world and the King were suddenly at her feet, and perhaps it is hardly surprising that she should have paid little attention to the duties and responsibilities of her new dignity. Pampered and petted by a doting husband, flattered and fawned upon by the place-seeking multitudes, heedless and shallow by nature, she proceeded to concentrate her considerable energies on indulging a seemingly insatiable appetite for pleasure.

The Queen's behaviour may have been understandable, but it was not very wise. As long as the King remained besotted and as long as her old playmates were kept sweet with positions in her household, there seemed small danger of her past catching up with her – who, after all, would be so foolish as to kill the goose which was laying so many delicious golden eggs? – but it was not only Katherine's past which made her vulnerable. Assisted by the King's timely infatuation, the Howards had climbed back into power and favour over the dead body of Thomas Cromwell and were now unashamedly enjoying the sweets of victory. Howard arrogance alone would have made them unpopular, but they and their party also represented the reactionary right wing in both religion and politics, and as such they were feared and resented by the progressive faction, which advocated a far more radical programme of religious reform than the King had yet been prepared to sanction. The progressives, who numbered many able and ambitious men among their ranks, watched angrily as the Queen's relations dug themselves in around the throne, and meditated a counter-stroke. The flighty Howard queen, symbol and source of the family's ascendancy, offered a natural target for the family's enemies, and unfortunately Katherine was to demonstrate that, like her cousin Anne Boleyn, she had quite a useful talent for making enemies on her own account. She was jealous of the Princess Mary and quarrelled with her, thus offending the Princess's friends. She had surrounded herself with old friends from Lambeth days: Alice Restwold, Joan Bulmer, Katherine Tylney and Margaret Morton were all found places as chamberers and were so intimate with the Queen that other, more superior ladies of the bedchamber complained they were being ousted and ignored. Even more foolishly, the Queen had also welcomed another old friend, giving Francis Dereham, of all people, the post of private secretary and usher of the chamber. Worse still, Katherine had taken another lover. Within six months of her marriage she was casting languishing glances at Master Thomas Culpeper, gentleman of the privy chamber and yet another distant cousin. Soon, with an almost incredible lack of the most basic kind of common sense, she was sending him presents and snatching secret meetings, with the connivance of Lady Rochford (widow of Anne Boleyn's brother George), who seems to have possessed all the instincts of a natural procuress.

In the summer of 1541 the King made his long-postponed visit to the North, progressing with great pomp and splendour as far as York, and all along the route Thomas Culpeper was being smuggled up the backstairs to keep late-night rendezvous with the Queen. Just as at Lambeth, it was impossible to keep this sort of thing quiet. Some people's suspicions had been aroused simply by seeing the way Katherine looked at Culpeper. Others had begun to notice that the Queen never seemed to go to bed and was curiously unanxious for company in the evenings, admitting only Lady Rochford and her friend Katherine Tylney to her apartments. By the time the Court returned to London at the end of October, gossip was running like wildfire through the household. Only the King remained in complacent ignorance – but not for much longer.

While the unwieldy cavalcade was still jolting on its homeward way, one John Lassells, whose sister Mary had once served the old Duchess of Norfolk both at Horsham and at Lambeth, had laid certain information before the Archbishop of Canterbury. Lassells was a convinced member of the reformist party, and so, though he was careful not to make it too obvious, was Thomas Cranmer. As he listened to John Lassells' detailed account of the Queen's shameless behaviour with her former music master and of her disgraceful goings-on with Francis Dereham in the dormitory at Lambeth, the Archbishop at once perceived its 'weight and importance'. It was, of course, just the sort of scandal which the anti-Howard faction had been waiting for. The problem was how best to pass it on to the King. Although, after fifteen months of marriage, Katherine had shown no signs of becoming pregnant, Henry's affections were still 'so marvellously set' upon her that no one really fancied the task of destroying his illusions. In the end, it fell to Cranmer, but even he, privileged old friend though he was, could not bring himself to break the news in person. Instead he wrote a letter, which he handed to the King in the chapel at Hampton Court, begging him to read it in private.

Henry's first reaction to the accusations against his wife was one of furious disbelief, and he ordered an enquiry to be put in hand immediately to discover those responsible for slandering the Queen. But Mary Lassells, now Mary Hall, confirmed her brother's story, and Manox and Dereham both admitted their past misdeeds, Dereham confessing that he had had intercourse with Katherine many times, 'both in his doublet and hose between the sheets and in naked bed'. Katherine herself began by denying everything, but in a private interview with Cranmer on 8 November she broke down and, between floods of hysterical tears, told him how Dereham had lain with her and used her 'in such sort as a man doth use his wife many and sundry times'. In a confession addressed to the King, she threw herself on his mercy and as much blame as possible on others, beseeching her husband 'to consider the subtle persuasions of young men and the ignorance and frailness of young women'. True, she had succumbed to the flattery of Manox and had allowed Francis Dereham to procure her 'to his vicious purpose'; but, this ingenuous document continued: 'I was so desirous to be taken unto your Grace's favour and so blinded with the desire of worldly glory that I could not, nor had grace, to consider how great a fault it was to conceal my former faults from your Majesty, considering that I intended ever during my life to be faithful and true unto your Majesty after.'

So far there had been no suggestion of adultery – Dereham utterly denied any misconduct with the Queen since her marriage – and so far the worst crime Katherine could legally be charged with was bigamy. But although she admitted having called Dereham 'husband' during the period of their intimacy, she refused, from either pride or pig-headedness, to admit the existence of any pre-contract or engagement between them. Nevertheless, it looked as if she might still escape with divorce and social disgrace. Then the Council's bloodhounds picked up the scent of Thomas Culpeper, and the whole complexion of the case was changed.

Questioned on 'the matter now come forth concerning Culpeper', Katherine admitted the clandestine meetings; she confessed to having called him her 'little sweet fool' and giving him a cap and a ring, but she denied 'upon her oath' that she had ever gone to bed with him. Characteristically, she accused Culpeper of having pestered her with his attentions and blamed Lady Rochford for encouraging him and deliberately acting as an *agent provocateur*. Lady Rochford, naturally enough, maintained that she had performed the services of go-between on the Queen's explicit orders, adding that she thought Culpeper *had* known the Queen carnally, 'considering all the things that she hath heard and seen between them'.

Despite the Council's best efforts, actual adultery was never conclusively proved, though the presumption that the King had been systematically cuckolded must be pretty strong, and, in any case, Culpeper confessed that 'he intended and meant to do ill with the Queen and in likewise the Queen so minded to do with him'. This was quite enough to condemn them both, and when a friend of Francis Dereham's conveniently remembered that individual's once saying he was sure he might still marry the Queen if the King were dead, that was enough to condemn him too. Under the 1534 Treason Act, evidence of evil intent against the Crown was all that was needed for a conviction.

Dereham and Culpeper were tried together at the beginning of December and executed together ten days later, but Katherine was not even accorded the courtesy of a trial. Parliament met in January, 1542, and proceeded to pass an Act of Attainder against the Queen, setting forth her treason and carefully locking the stable door after the horse had been stolen. In future, it was laid down that if the King should take a fancy to a woman, innocently believing her to be 'a pure and clean maid' when proof to the contrary was later forthcoming, or if such a woman coupled herself with her sovereign lord without first disclosing the existence of her unchaste life, then every such offence would be deemed and adjudged high treason – a provision which, as the cynics did not fail to point out, was likely to limit the monarch's field of choice pretty severely.

Katherine was brought by water from Syon House, where she had spent the last weeks of her life, to the Tower on 10 February and two days later was warned to 'dispose of her soul and prepare for death'. Although so weak that she had to be helped up the steps to the scaffold, she died well. The sixteenth century considered it important to die well, with dignity and proper repentance for one's sins – not merely for the sake of the soul's salvation, but 'to leave a good opinion in the people's minds' – and the Queen had summoned up sufficient reserves of courage and self-command to enable her to make a final appearance worthy of a Howard lady.

Katherine Howard was an extreme, but by no means untypical example of the way in which her world regarded its womenfolk as pawns in the game of high politics. Silly, feckless and over-sexed, she'd been incapable of meeting the demands made upon her and had become the inevitable victim of a system which ruthlessly eliminated its failures.

The King's self-esteem had been grievously wounded by his young wife's betrayal. Back in the days when Anne Boleyn was being accused of adultery on a far grander scale than poor Katherine's, Eustace Chapuys remarked of Henry that he had never seen prince or man who wore his horns more pleasantly. But things were different now, and Chapuys, still in England, still observing the antics of the islanders with a coldly clinical eye, probably came near the truth when he wrote that the King's case resembled very much 'that of the woman who cried more bitterly at the loss of her tenth husband than she had on the death of the other nine put together ... the reason being that she had never buried one of them without being sure of the next, but that after the tenth husband she had no other in view, hence her sorrow and her lamentations.'

All the same, rather to some people's surprise, the King did marry again, and in a quiet ceremony at Hampton Court on 12 July 1543 the widowed Lady Latimer of Snape Hall became the sixth woman to stand beside her sovereign lord and vow to 'take thee, Henry, to my wedded husband, to have and to hold from this day forward, for better for worse, for richer for poorer, in sickness and in health, to be bonair and buxom in bed and at board, till death us do part'.

If Henry had been seeking a loyal and sympathetic companion for his declining years, he could hardly have made a better choice. Lady Latimer, born Katherine Parr, had already been twice married to men much older than herself and been twice widowed. At thirty-one she was still a pretty woman, but more to the point she was also a mature, well-educated and thoughtful woman, experienced in the arts of managing elderly husbands. In the words of the anonymous author of *The Spanish Chronicle*, she was 'quieter than any of the young wives the King had had, and as she knew more of the world, she always got on pleasantly with the King and had no caprices'.

The new Queen and her family were no strangers to royal circles. Her sister Anne was married to William Herbert, one of the Esquires of the Body, and her brother William was making a notable career for himself in the royal service, having just been appointed to the key post of Lord Warden of the Scottish Marches. Their mother had been one of Catherine of Aragon's ladies, and Katherine had spent her earliest years at Court, being one of the hand-picked young girls chosen to share the Princess Mary's lessons under the direction of Luis Vives. Unlike her immediate predecessor, Katherine Parr had been carefully brought up and was not only aware of her responsibilities but eager to fulfil them. She was to prove an excellent wife and a kind and conscientious stepmother, creating a comfortable domestic enclave at Court where the royal family could be almost cosy. But her talents were not confined to the home. Henry's sixth Queen, like his first, was a woman of trained intelligence and shrewd political sense. Her influence rapidly became a factor to be reckoned with, and, in one case at least, it was to have incalculable consequences for England.

CHAPTER SIX

When Women
Become Such Clerks

Under the beneficent rule of Queen Katherine Parr, scholarly pursuits once more became fashionable at Court. Following in the footsteps of pious and serious-minded ladies like Margaret Beaufort and Catherine of Aragon, Katherine Parr took an informed interest in intellectual matters and was a lively patron of the New Learning. She encouraged the Princess Mary to exercise her mind and make use of her Latin by embarking on a translation of Erasmus's paraphrase of the Gospel of St John, and she is generally credited with helping to secure the appointment of John Cheke, lecturer in Greek and Fellow of Margaret Beaufort's foundation of St John's College Cambridge, as principal tutor to the six-year-old Prince of Wales. But more important – more important indeed than the Queen would ever know – was her determination to ensure that the Princess Elizabeth should receive the same high standard of education as her brother and sister.

Henry's younger daughter was ten years old now, a pale, red-headed girl, becoming a little withdrawn and inclined to stand stiffly on her dignity. Since Anne Boleyn's disgrace, the motherless Elizabeth had been living with her household staff in one or other of the numerous royal manors scattered around the Home Counties, usually sharing an establishment with either her brother or sister. She was not neglected in any obvious sense. Her father was quite fond of her when he remembered her existence, and she took her place as a member of the family on state occasions – she'd made her debut at Prince Edward's christening and had been present at the official celebrations to welcome

Anne of Cleves – but until the advent of Katherine Parr there had been no influential personage at Court with the will or the power to take a special interest in her welfare, and her upbringing had been left pretty well entirely in the hands of her governess.

Katherine Parr was fully aware of the dangers and difficulties attached to the position of Henry VIII's sixth wife, but being a woman of spirit and strong principles she intended not only to survive but to make a success of the task to which she believed God had called her. It was part of her policy from the beginning to work to unite the royal family and to establish good relations with her stepchildren, thus creating a power base for herself which would be independent of any rival faction. This was intelligent thinking and an undertaking for which the Queen, with her warm outgoing personality, was especially suited. She and Mary already knew and respected each other, and now they became firm friends. The Queen saw to it that there was always a warm welcome for the Princess at Court, and when Mary went back to her Essex home, they corresponded regularly (often in Latin), exchanged presents and lent one another small services or servants with special skills.

Katherine experienced no difficulty either in gaining the trust of young Prince Edward. The boy was genuinely fond of her and began calling her 'mother' almost at once. Edward and Mary were both figures of political importance whose goodwill would undoubtedly be a valuable asset; but it was Elizabeth, bastard of a notorious adulteress, without friends or influence or any apparent future, who became the Queen's particular protégée. Katherine brought the proud, lonely little girl to Court, gave her apartments next to her own at Greenwich and Whitehall and took pains to draw her into the family circle. It was almost certainly Katherine's doing that William Grindal, another Cambridge scholar, was appointed tutor to the Princess, and she continued to keep a careful watch over the child's progress. Elizabeth, always responsive to affection and fiercely loyal in her friendships, repaid her stepmother with love. Her earliest surviving letter was written to Katherine in July 1544 in Italian – probably as an exercise – and at the end of the year she presented the Queen with a laborious translation from the French of a long and exceedingly dull poem by Margaret of Navarre, bound in an elaborately embroidered cover worked by herself.

In the summer of 1544 the King departed on his last warlike adventure abroad, creating his wife Regent in his absence – an honour not accorded to a consort since the days of Catherine of Aragon. Unlike her predecessor, Katherine Parr was not called upon to fight a war on the home front, but she was left an almost equally awesome responsibility in the guardianship of Prince Edward – his father's pride and joy and England's Treasure. While the King was away, the Queen gathered her new family round her at Hampton Court, sending regular bulletins to France about the health of 'my lord Prince' and his sisters. Her domesticating influence was already being noted in the outside world, a new factor on the English political scene and worthy of mention in ambassadors' despatches, while at home she was winning golden opinions among the liberal intelligentsia. Every day at Court was like a Sunday, enthused one of the scholars patronized by Katherine, adding that this was something 'hitherto unheard of, especially in a royal palace'. Nicholas Udall, master at Eton College and editor of the volume of translations to which Mary had contributed, wrote in his preface that it was now no strange thing to hear gentlewomen use grave and substantial talk in Greek or Latin with their husbands in godly matters. 'It is now no news in England', he went on, 'to see young damsels in noble houses and in the Courts of princes, instead of cards and other instruments of vain trifling, to have continually in their hands either psalms, homilies or other devout meditations.'

This spreading interest in 'godly matters' was a direct, if unintentional, result of Henry's quarrel with the Pope and had recently received a vital stimulus by the publication of the so-called Great Bible – based on Tyndale's and Coverdale's translations – which went through seven editions between the years 1539 and 1541. Its effect on an increasingly literate and sophisticated public was electric. To the average concerned and educated layman it meant that he was now, for the first time, in a position to study and interpret the Word of God for himself, and this in turn led to the exhilarating realization that it was possible for an individual to make his own approaches to the Almighty without having to depend entirely on the priest to act as intermediary. This was an experience in which the women could share; indeed, in many households, it was the women who took the lead. To the woman trapped in a loveless marriage, to all those women who had failed to find fulfilment within the narrow limits of home and family, restless souls seeking an outlet for frustrated emotional and intellectual energies, the discovery of the Scriptures, and with it a whole new world of delights in which the spirit could find its own refreshment, brought a sense of release and excitement which transformed thousands of lives.

In the most important household in the land, the women were also taking the lead. Queen Katherine Parr was known to favour the so-called New Faith, which laid great stress on the importance of private devotion while playing down the organized, sacramental aspects of religious observance. She had gathered a number of like-minded ladies round her, and together they spent much of their time studying and discussing the Gospels and listening to discourses by such fashionably advanced preachers as Nicholas Ridley, Hugh Latimer and Nicholas Shaxton. Katherine's circle included her sister, Anne Herbert, and her stepdaughter, Elizabeth Tyrwhit; Joan Denny, wife of one of the King's favourite gentlemen of the Privy Chamber; the outspoken young Duchess of Suffolk, the Countess of Sussex, Lady Fitzwilliam, Lady Lane, and Jane Dudley and Anne Seymour, Countess of Hertford, whose husbands were both leading members of the progressive party at Court.

But, in spite of their privileged position, the Queen and her friends were treading on dangerous ground, for, the break with Rome notwithstanding, England was still, in the early 1540s, to all practical intents and purposes a Catholic country, with observance of all the basic tenets of the Catholic faith still legally enforceable. The conservative faction had suffered a serious set-back over the Katherine Howard affair, but they remained a force to be reckoned with, and right-wing bishops like Bonner of London and Gardiner of Winchester were becoming increas-ingly disturbed by the spread of heresy, especially in London and the south-east.

The bishops knew all about the Queen's study groups and strongly suspected that she was giving active encouragement not only to subversive elements within the Church but to those outside it who were beginning to challenge the priesthood to show scriptural authority for their claim to represent the only channel through which the laity could hope to receive divine grace. Gardiner, Bonner and their supporters on the Council had no doubt who to blame for the growing strength of radical religious views in high places, and there was, of course, a good deal of personal animosity involved as well. The right-wingers were jealous of Katherine's influence with the King and his children, and although the Queen herself was always tactful, some of her followers were not. The Duchess of Suffolk, for example, had named her pet spaniel 'Gardiner' in a deliber-ately provocative gesture and made no secret of her low opinion of his Grace of Winchester and all his works; while Lady Hert-ford, arrogant and quarrelsome, never experienced any diffi-culty in getting herself disliked.

Since her marriage the Queen had undoubtedly moved steadily further towards Protestantism, and in the summer of 1546 her enemies at last saw an opportunity to pounce. In her little book of prayers and meditations, *The Lamentation of a Sin-ner*, which had recently been circulating in manuscript form, Katherine reminded her own sex that: 'if they be women married, they learn of St Paul to be obedient to their husbands, and to keep silence in the congregation, and to learn of their husbands at home'. Unfortunately, there was to be an occasion towards the end of June 1546 when the Queen failed to follow this excellent advice – at least according to the story later told by John Foxe in his best-selling *Book of Martyrs*. Henry's danc-ing days were over now, and it was his wife's habit to sit with him in the evenings and endeavour to entertain him and take his mind off the pain of his ulcerated legs by inaugurating a discussion on some serious topic, which inevitably meant some religious topic. On this particular occasion, Katherine seems to have allowed her enthusiasm to run away with her, and the King was provoked into grumbling to Stephen Gardiner: 'A good hearing it is, when women become such clerks, and a thing much to my comfort to come in mine old days to be taught by my wife.'

This, of course, was Gardiner's cue to warn his sovereign lord that he had reason to believe the Queen was deliberately under-mining the stability of the state by fomenting heresy of the most odious kind and encouraging the lieges to question the wisdom of their prince's government. So much so, that the Council was 'bold to affirm that the greatest subject in this land, speaking those words that she did speak and defending likewise those arguments that she did defend, had with impartial justice by law deserved death'. Henry was all attention. Anything which touched the assurance of his own estate was not to be treated lightly, and he authorized an immediate enquiry into the ortho-doxy of the Queen's household, agreeing that if any evidence of subversion were forthcoming, charges could be brought against Katherine herself.

Gardiner and his ally on the Council, the Lord Chancellor Thomas Wriothesley, planned to attack the Queen through her ladies and believed they possessed a valuable weapon in the person of Anne Kyme, better known by her maiden name of Anne Askew, a notorious heretic already convicted and con-demned. Anne, a truculent and argumentative young woman who came from a well-known Lincolnshire family, had left her husband and come to London to seek a divorce. Quoting fluently from the Scriptures, she claimed that her marriage was no longer valid in the sight of God, for had not St Paul written: 'If a faithful woman have an unbelieving husband, which will not tarry with her she may leave him'? (Thomas Kyme was an old-fashioned Catholic who objected strongly to his wife's Bible-punching propensities.)

Anne failed to get her divorce, but her zeal, her sharp tongue and her lively wit soon made her a well-known figure in Protestant circles. Inevitably she soon came up against the law, and in March 1546 she was arrested on suspicion of heresy, specifically on a charge of denying the Real Presence in the sacrament of the altar. Pressed by Bishop Bonner on this vital point, Anne hesitated and was finally persuaded to sign a confession which amounted to an only slightly qualified statement of orthodox belief. A few days later she was released from gaol and went home to Lincolnshire – not to her husband but to her brother Sir Francis Askew.

Throughout that spring the conservative counter-attack gathered momentum, and by early summer a vigorous anti-heresy drive was in progress. At the end of May Thomas Kyme and his wife were summoned to appear before the Council. Although not proved, it's probable that the initiative for this move came from Kyme himself. Anne had refused to obey the order of the Court of Chancery to return to him, nor is it likely that he wanted her back. At the same time, he was in an invidious position, deserted and defied by his wife and unable to marry again. It cannot have failed to occur to him that only Anne's death would finally solve his problems. Armed with a royal warrant and backed up by the Bishop of Lincoln (who had a long score to settle with Anne), Thomas Kyme forcibly removed her from her brother's protection and carried her off to London.

The Council's summons was ostensibly about the matrimonial issue, and Kyme was soon dismissed, but Anne, 'for that she was very obstinate and heady in reasoning of matters of religion, wherein she avowed herself to be of a naughty opinion', was committed to Newgate prison to face renewed heresy charges. All through the following week determined efforts were made to wring from her a second and more complete recantation. The bishops were not anxious to make martyrs – retractions, especially from the better-known Protestants, would obviously be more valuable for propaganda purposes – but Anne was not to be caught a second time. When Stephen

Gardiner tried his charm on her, begging her to believe he was her friend, concerned only with her soul's health, she retorted that that was just the attitude adopted by Judas 'when he unfriendly betrayed Christ'. Any lingering doubts and fears had passed. She knew now, with serene certainty, what Christ wanted from her, and she was ready to give it. At her trial on 28 June she flatly rejected the existence of any priestly miracle in the eucharist. 'As for that ye call your God, it is a piece of bread. For a more proof thereof ... let it but lie in the box three months and it will be mouldy.' After that, there could be no question of the verdict, and sentence of death by burning was duly passed on this self-confessed and obstinate heretic.

Anne Askew is an interesting example of an educated, highly-intelligent, passionate woman destined to become the victim of the society in which she lived – a woman who could not accept her circumstances but fought an angry, hopeless battle against them. She was unquestionably sincere in her religious convictions – to what extent she also used them unconsciously to sublimate tensions and frustrations which might otherwise have been unbearable, we can only speculate. To Thomas Wriothesley the interesting thing about her was the fact that she was known to have close connections with the Court. Two of her brothers were in the royal service, and she was friendly with John Lassells – the same who had betrayed Katherine Howard five years before. It's highly probable that Anne had attended some of the Biblical study sessions in the Queen's apartments, and she was certainly acquainted with some of the Queen's ladies. If it could now be shown that any of these ladies – perhaps even the Queen herself – had been in touch with her since her recent arrest; if it could be proved that they had been encouraging her to stand firm in her heresy, then the Lord Chancellor would have ample excuse for an attack on Katherine Parr.

Anne was therefore transferred to the Tower, where she received a visit from Wriothesley and his henchman Sir Richard Rich, the Solicitor General, but the interview proved a disappointment. She denied having received any visits while she had been in prison, and no one had willed her to stick to her opinions. Her maid had been given ten shillings by a man in a blue coat who said that Lady Hertford had sent it, and eight shillings by another man in a violet coat who said it came from Lady Denny, but whether this was true or not she didn't know, it was only what her maid had told her.

Convinced that Anne could have given them a long list of highly-placed secret sympathizers, and infuriated perhaps by her air of stubborn righteousness, Wriothesley ordered her to be stretched on the rack. This was not only illegal without a proper authorization from the Privy Council, it was unheard of to apply torture to a woman, let alone a gentlewoman like Anne Askew with friends in the outside world, and the Lieutenant of the Tower hastily dissociated himself from the whole proceeding. As a result, there followed a quite unprecedented scene, with the Lord Chancellor of England stripping off his gown and personally turning the handle of the rack. It was a foolish thing to do. Anne told him nothing more, if indeed there was anything to tell, and, since the story of her constancy soon got about, he'd only succeeded in turning her into a popular heroine.

The plot against the Queen fizzled out, largely due to the King's intervention. He took care that Katherine should receive advance warning of what was being planned for her and gave her the opportunity to explain that of course she had never for one moment intended to lay down the law to him, her lord and master, her only anchor, supreme head and governor here on earth. It was preposterous – against the ordinance of nature – for any woman to presume to teach her husband; it was she who must be taught by him. As for herself, if she had ever seemed bold enough to argue, it had not been to maintain her own opinions but to encourage discussion so that he might 'pass away the weariness of his present infirmity' and she might profit by hearing his learned discourse! Satisfied, the King embraced his wife, and an affecting reconciliation took place.

If any real evidence of treasonable heresy had been uncovered in the Queen's household – if Henry had seriously suspected that

Katherine was connected with any group which planned to challenge his own mandate from Heaven – then this story might have ended differently. As it was, he'd apparently been sufficiently irritated to feel that it would do her no harm to be taught a lesson, to be given a fright and a sharp warning not to meddle in matters which were no concern of outsiders, however privileged. Katherine, with her usual good sense, took the warning to heart, and there's no mention of any further theological disputations, even amicable ones, between husband and wife.

The Queen was unable to save Anne Askew, but her martyrdom on 16 July 1546 marked the end of the conservative resurgence, and by the time of the old King's death in the following January the progressive party was once more taking the lead.

The Court of a motherless child-King – Edward was nine years old when he succeeded – offered little scope for feminine influence, but the feminine element could not be disregarded since there were now no fewer than ten Tudor women standing in direct line of succession. Apart from Henry's two daughters, three nieces had survived him – Margaret Douglas, daughter of his elder sister's second marriage, and Frances and Eleanor Brandon, children of his younger sister and her second husband, Charles Brandon, Duke of Suffolk. Frances had married Henry Grey, Marquis of Dorset, and produced three daughters, Jane, Katherine and Mary, now aged respectively nine, seven and two; while Eleanor had been matched with Henry Clifford, heir to the Earl of Cumberland. Eleanor had lost two sons in infancy, but a daughter, Margaret, survived.

There was one other great-niece, born in 1542, Mary Stuart, Queen of Scotland, grand-daughter of Margaret Tudor and only living descendant of the Tudor–Stuart alliance forged by Henry VII nearly half a century before. That alliance had since been through numerous vicissitudes, but in the 1540s Anglo-Scottish relations were at an especially low ebb. After his overwhelming victory over his neighbours at the battle of Solway Moss, Henry VIII had attempted to repeat his father's diplomacy by arranging a marriage between the infant Queen of Scots and his own son, but negotiations had foundered on the rocks of English insensitivity and Scottish suspicion, and now Scotland had once again turned back to her ancient ally across the Channel. In the spring of 1548, the five-year-old Queen was spirited away to France to be betrothed to the Dauphin, while Scotland was ruled in her name by her mother, that tough, capable Frenchwoman Mary of Guise. Mary Stuart was destined to cast a long shadow over the English political scene, but in 1548 her defection represented no more than a tiresome setback for the new government's plans for solving the Scottish problem – Fotheringay, after all, was still nearly forty years away.

The fact that the English royal House now consisted almost exclusively of a gaggle of women and little girls, was politically and dynastically unfortunate, but everyone naturally hoped that the new King would be luckier than his father when it came to getting sons. Everyone hoped that young Edward would grow uneventfully to manhood and quickly replenish the stock of Tudor boys; but equally no one could deny that so far Tudor boys had shown a very poor survival record and that England's chances of having a woman ruler before the end of the century must be reckoned high.

By an Act of Parliament passed in 1544, Henry VIII had reinstated both his daughters to their places in the succession. In the event of his son dying without heirs, and failing any children by his own sixth marriage, the crown would pass first to Mary and then to Elizabeth. Neither of the princesses had been relegitimized by the 1544 Act – the awkward question of their legitimacy had simply been ignored. After his own children, the King, using the powers granted him by Parliament in 1536 to dispose of the Crown by Will, had arbitrarily passed over the senior, Scottish branch of the family represented by Mary Stuart and Margaret Douglas, in favour of the so-called Suffolk line – that is to the descendants of his sister Mary Brandon. This was to prove a deadly legacy for the Suffolk girls and confused the whole vital issue of the succession for a generation.

Katherine Parr had been left no say in the regency and no further share in the upbringing of her stepson. Until Edward married, however, she remained the first lady in the land (much to the annoyance of the new Lord Protector's wife) and was generously provided for financially. In his Will Henry had paid tribute to her great love, obedience, chastity of life and wisdom and had bequeathed her three thousand pounds in plate, jewels, household goods and apparel, and a thousand pounds in money, in addition to the jointure already granted by Parliament. Katherine was now in the happy position of being free to arrange her life as she chose, and shortly after Henry's death she moved to her dower manor at Chelsea, taking with her the thirteen-year-old Elizabeth who, it had been agreed, should remain with the Queen until she had completed her education. The establishment at Chelsea was presently joined by young Jane Grey, eldest of King Henry's English great-nieces, thus maintaining the time-honoured custom of using a great lady's household as a finishing-school for girls.

If the Queen was disappointed at being excluded from the councils of state, she at least had the satisfaction of knowing that power had passed into the hands of those who thought as she did on matters of religion. The King's uncle, Edward Seymour, Earl of Hertford, now raised to the dignity of Duke of Somerset and officially styled Lord Protector, could be relied upon to push through the programme of reform long desired by Katherine and her friends. She might no longer be at the centre of affairs, but the King was known to be very fond of his stepmother, and she still exerted a good deal of influence. In any case, she scarcely had time to feel dull and out of things, for an exciting development in her private life soon began to occupy most of her attention.

Bereavement being a commonplace affliction for both sexes, the writers of conduct-books devoted a lot of space to the subject. All were agreed that a widow, and especially a young widow, could not be too careful. She was bound to become a target for gossip, since the unchastity of widows was proverbial, and would be considered fair game by a certain type of man. A wealthy widow must also bear in mind the danger of falling a prey to fortune-hunters. She should therefore live as quietly as possible, scrupulously avoiding all mixed gatherings, and take some older woman of unassailable virtue to be her constant companion; better still, she should return to her parents or make a home with her husband's kin.

On the desirability of re-marriage, opinion was divided, some stricter moralists holding that the widow should devote the rest of her life to bringing up her children, to good works and piously revering her late husband's memory. Others, following the teachings of St Paul, believed that, after a decent interval of mourning, a nubile widow should re-marry, as this would be her best protection against temptation to a life of sin and consequent damnation, and urged her to place herself in her family's hands regarding the choice of a second husband. In spite of the fact that most pundits advised their readers against marrying a widow, for 'she will always be either praising or praying for her first husband', the vast majority did re-marry, often within months of the funeral. Whatever her private inclinations, it took an exceedingly strong-minded lady to face the difficulties of life on her own, especially if she had young children to think of, or to withstand family pressures and the deeply-ingrained prejudices of society against the independent single woman.

A rich widow, of course, never lacked for suitors, and the richest, most desirable widow in the realm was no exception to this rule. Within a very few weeks of King Henry's death, the Queen Dowager was being courted by Thomas Seymour, younger brother of the Lord Protector, and three months later they were married. This was not quite so precipitate as it looked, for the couple were old acquaintances and had, in fact, been planning to marry at the time of Katherine's second widowhood, in the brief period before Henry declared his interest. As the Queen wrote to her fiancé:

I would not have you think that this mine honest good will toward you to proceed from any sudden motion of passion; for, as truly as God is God, my mind was fully bent, the other time I was at liberty, to marry you before any man I know. Howbeit, God withstood my will therein most vehemently for a time, and ... made that possible which seemed to me most impossible; that was, made me renounce utterly mine own will and to follow His will most willingly.... I can say nothing but as my lady of Suffolk saith, 'God is a marvellous man.'

Now that she was at last free to please herself, it was natural enough that Katherine should have been impatient to snatch a chance of personal happiness. Unlike so many of her contemporaries she had not been prematurely aged by constant child-bearing, but at thirty-four there was no time to lose and, unwisely as it turned out, the pious, high-minded Queen allowed herself to be swept off her feet.

Thomas Seymour, now created Baron Seymour of Sudeley and given the office of Lord Admiral, was a fine figure of a man, with plenty of breezy surface charm – 'fierce in courage, courtly in fashion; in personage stately, in voice magnificent, but somewhat empty of matter'. He was also a vain, greedy, selfish man, consumed with ambition but lacking any political judgement and obsessively jealous of his elder brother. Unknown to Katherine, his whirlwind courtship of the Queen Dowager had been the first step in a calculated campaign of self-advancement, and their marriage, which took place secretly, was not popular in certain quarters. However, the little King was graciously pleased to give it his blessing, and by midsummer the Admiral had moved in with his wife at Chelsea, where his boisterous, loud-voiced presence rapidly dispelled any resemblance to a girls' boarding-school. His habit of bursting in on the Princess Elizabeth and her maids in the early morning, still in his nightshirt and slippers, to tickle her and smack her familiarly on the behind, would certainly not have been tolerated in such an establishment and was regarded with strong disapproval by the Princess's governess. Katherine, who sometimes joined in these merry romps herself, made light of Mrs Ashley's complaints; but Mrs Ashley, whose sharp ears had already picked up the whispers that if my lord 'might have had his own will' he would have married the Lady Elizabeth before he married the Queen, continued to worry rather ineffectually about the situation and to dread that her princess would be 'evilly spoken of'.

Thomas Seymour never indulged his taste for horse-play with the other young girl living under his wife's roof, but he was taking a close interest in her future. The provisions of her great-uncle's Will had dramatically increased the political impor-tance of Lady Jane Grey, and the Admiral, with his usual optimism, saw no reason why this should not be turned to his own advantage. He therefore opened negotiations with the Marquess of Dorset, and, as that gentleman later admitted, 'certain covenants' were entered into. Put rather more bluntly, Dorset agreed to sell his daughter's wardship and marriage for the sum of two thousand pounds. The Admiral, he was told, would arrange to marry the Lady Jane to the King, and on this understanding the bargain was struck and several hundred pounds handed over on account.

No one, naturally, thought it necessary to consult the Lady Jane about these interesting plans, nor would she have expected it. At nine years old, Jane Grey was absorbed in her lessons and, encouraged by the Queen, who had become very fond of her, was already beginning to develop into a notable scholar and paragon of Protestant piety. Had her opinion been asked, Jane would undoubtedly have chosen to remain with the Queen and the Lord Admiral. She didn't get on with her parents and was bullied at home, but at Chelsea she was petted and praised, her diligence and 'towardness' were openly discussed and admired and her brilliant prospects whispered over by the ladies of the household. But for Jane, as for Katherine Parr, this happy time was destined to be tragically brief.

In the early spring of 1548, after three barren marriages, Katherine knew herself to be pregnant, and perhaps for that reason she was no longer quite so complaisant about her hus-band's playful attentions to her stepdaughter. Matters came to a head one day when she came upon the two of them locked in an embrace which was not in the least playful, and as a result Elizabeth was sent with her servants to pay a protracted visit to Sir Anthony and Lady Denny at their house at Cheshunt. What-ever her private feelings of hurt and betrayal, Katherine was very careful to avoid any appearance of an open breach. She knew that gossip, once started, would be unstoppable and would cause irreparable damage to them all, but especially to Elizabeth. So the Queen and the Princess parted affectionately, and a penitent Elizabeth showed that she appreciated the tact and generosity of the woman to whom she already owed so much. 'Although I could not be plentiful in giving thanks for the manifold kindness received at your Highness' hands,' she wrote from Cheshunt, 'yet I am something to be borne withal, for truly I was replete with sorrow to depart from your Highness, especially leaving you undoubtful of health.' Luckily everyone knew that the Queen, now in the sixth month of an uncomfortable pregnancy, and the Admiral were planning to spend the summer on their Gloucestershire estates, and in the general business of packing up it had been possible to contrive Elizabeth's move without arousing curiosity.

Any unpleasantness between husband and wife was quickly smoothed over. Katherine knew that, like any other wife, she must expect a man's fancy to stray from time to time, and probably she was a good deal more worried by her husband's ill-advised political activities. She supported him loyally in his personal quarrels with the Protector, but she was far too intelligent and politically experienced herself not to see the danger of his wild, whirling schemes for bringing down his brother's government and seizing control of the King. Very likely she was pinning her hopes on the coming child. If Thomas Seymour had a son to consider, it might steady him and help him to settle down and forget his various grievances. The baby had quickened now, and Katherine wrote from Hanworth in Middlesex, another of her dower houses, to her 'sweetheart and loving husband' who had been delayed in London on business: 'I have given your little knave your blessing, who like an honest man stirred apace after and before; for Mary Odell being abed with me had laid her hand upon my belly to feel it stir. It hath stirred these three days every morning and evening, so that I trust when you come, it will make you some pastime.'

Katherine's baby, a girl christened Mary, was born at Sudeley Castle on 30 August, and the long-suffering Lord Protector sent his brother a kind note of congratulation. 'We are right glad to understand by your letters', he wrote, 'that the Queen, your bedfellow, hath had a happy hour; and, escaping all danger, hath made you the father of so pretty a daughter.' But even as this letter was being written, Katherine had developed the dreaded symptoms of childbed fever, and within a week she was dead. She was buried in the chapel at Sudeley with all the pomp due to a Queen Dowager of England, with Jane Grey, a diminutive, lonely figure clad in deepest black, acting as chief mourner for the only person ever to show her disinterested kindness.

In the domestic confusion which followed Katherine's death, Jane was summoned home by her parents. She could scarcely remain in a bachelor household with no lady of rank to chaperone her, and the Dorsets were, in any case, growing restive. More than a year had gone by with no sign of any of Thomas Seymour's 'fair promises' being fulfilled, and the Marquess now showed every indication of trying to wriggle out of his undertaking. Jane, he wrote, was too young to rule herself without a guide and, for want of a bridle, might take too much head and forget all the good behaviour she had learned from the late Queen. He and his wife both felt strongly that she should remain under her mother's eye to be 'framed and ruled towards virtue' and her mind addressed to humility, soberness and obedience.

This sudden access of concern for their daughter's welfare imperfectly concealed a ruthless determination to sell her to the highest bidder, and the Dorsets were beginning to wonder if, after all, it might not be wiser to settle for a match with the Lord Protector's son which had already been tentatively discussed. But Thomas Seymour had no intention of giving up his claim to the Lady Jane. He told Dorset that he intended to retain the services of all the late Queen's ladies, 'the maids that waited at large and other women being about her Grace in her lifetime'. As well as this, his own mother was coming to take charge of the household and would be 'as dear unto her [Jane] as though she were her own daughter'. He repeated his promises that if he could once get the King at liberty, he would ensure that his Majesty married no other than Jane, and he agreed to pay over another five hundred of the agreed two thousand pounds purchase money. Lord Dorset was not proof against this form of persuasion, and some time in October, round about her eleventh birthday, Jane was returned to the custody of the Lord Admiral.

The Lord Admiral was now actively considering his own marital future, and a rumour circulated briefly that he meant to marry Jane himself. Certainly he would not have been the first guardian to marry a wealthy or otherwise eligible ward – within two months of the death of his royal wife, the late Duke of Suffolk had married his ward, Katherine Willoughby, an heiress fully young enough to be his daughter – but the Admiral, it seemed, was setting his sights even higher. Gossip had already begun to link his name with the Princess Elizabeth, and it was being whispered that the real reason why he had kept Queen Katherine's maids together was to wait on the Princess once they were married.

In Elizabeth's household, now established at Hatfield in Hertfordshire, there was much excited speculation about the widower's intentions and how soon he might be expected to come courting. Mrs Ashley for one was already hearing wedding bells. She knew that the Admiral loved her princess 'but too well', and was he not 'the noblest man unmarried in this land'? But during those autumn months, while the Admiral conferred with her steward about the state of her finances, the number of servants she kept and the whereabouts of her landed property; while her governess sang his praises, and my lord sent her friendly messages at every opportunity, Elizabeth remained unresponsive. King Henry VIII might have failed in a father's first duty by leaving his daughters unbetrothed and un-protected against predators like Thomas Seymour, but even at fifteen years old Elizabeth Tudor could look after herself. The Admiral's flamboyant façade was convincing enough to deceive her steward and her governess, but Elizabeth knew or guessed just how flimsy that facade really was. She knew it was in the highest degree unlikely that the Protector and the Council would ever consent to her marriage with an adventurous younger son, and she knew that any attempt to marry without their consent would inevitably lead straight to disaster. In the privacy of the household she could not always conceal the warmth of her feelings for the Admiral – he was exactly the kind of bold, handsome fellow who would attract her to the end of her life – but in public her discretion was absolute, and she avoided all suggestion of a clandestine understanding with almost obsessive care.

It was as well that she did, for in January 1549 Thomas Seymour was committed to the Tower, evidence of his numerous 'disloyal practices' having become too blatant to be condoned any longer. On the day after his arrest, the government's investigators arrived at Hatfield, and over the next few weeks the Princess was subjected to a gruelling ordeal by interrogation. She was told it was being said that she was with child by the Lord Admiral and was invited 'to consider her honour and the peril that might ensue'. Embarrassing details of those early morning romps round the bed-curtains at Chelsea were dragged into the open, even the shameful reason why Queen Katherine had had to send her away to Cheshunt, but Elizabeth denied and continued to deny that she had ever for a moment contemplated marrying the Admiral or anyone else against the wishes of the King and his Council. Katherine Parr's good sense and her own courage, self-control and inborn political acumen had saved her from a disgrace which would have ruined her good name for ever and perhaps cost her her place in the succession, but the episode had provided a salutary lesson. Elizabeth learned early that the world was a hard and unforgiving place, and that the way to survive was at all costs to keep one's mouth shut and one's feelings to oneself. It was a lesson she never forgot. 'Her mind has no womanly weakness,' Roger Ascham, the most famous of her tutors, wrote of her later that same year, 'her perseverance is equal to that of a man, and her memory long keeps what it quickly picks up.'

Thomas Seymour was attainted of high treason and executed

on 20 March, leaving behind one innocent and often forgotten victim of his delusions of grandeur. Little Mary Seymour, stripped of her inheritance by her father's attainder, was dumped on the Duchess of Suffolk, once her mother's dear friend. But my lady of Suffolk, who always believed in speaking her mind, took a notably unsentimental view of the penniless infant and complained bitterly that she was being beggared by the cost of maintaining 'the Queen's child and her company'. Her ladyship made repeated efforts to extract an allowance for the baby's keep from the Lord Protector – the Queen's child was, after all, his niece – but whether or not she was successful is not recorded. Mary Seymour herself disappeared from the record before she was a year old and is generally believed to have died young, although there is a tradition, preserved by Agnes Strickland in her biography of Katherine Parr, that she survived to become the wife of Sir Edward Bushel, a gentleman of the household of James I's wife, Anne of Denmark.

CHAPTER SEVEN

Long Live Our Good Queen Mary

During Edward VI's brief reign, his elder sister and heir presumptive played no part in public affairs. Neither Mary nor Elizabeth was involved in the *coup d'état* which toppled the Lord Protector Somerset in the autumn of 1549 but, while Elizabeth paid regular visits to London to see the King, Mary avoided the Court. Under the new regent, John Dudley, Earl of Warwick, soon to become Duke of Northumberland, England was moving steadily to the left in religious matters. The Latin Mass had already been replaced by the new English communion service, and in 1552 a second and even more radical English Prayer Book came into use. To Mary, as to many others of her generation and temperament, the new ways were an abomination, and in the privacy of her household Mass continued to be celebrated. This led, inevitably, to confrontation. However much she tried to avoid the limelight, the Princess was a public figure and still a very popular one. Where she led, others would follow, and her conformity was therefore important.

For Mary the distress of being refused the consolations of her religion was equalled by her wretchedness over the widening rift between her brother and herself. Nevertheless, she resisted bravely. In the last resort, she told Edward at one of their rare meetings, 'there are two things only, soul and body. My soul I offer to God, and my body to your Majesty's service. May it please you to take away my life rather than the old religion.' Embarrassed, the boy made a 'gentle answer', and one of the standers-by tried to lower the temperature by pointing out that the King had no wish to constrain his sister's faith but merely willed her, as a subject, to obey his laws.

In the proceedings against the Princess, the Council, too, found themselves in a rather embarrassing position. Mary, like her mother, had powerful connections abroad, and already the Imperial ambassador was hinting at unpleasant consequences if his master's cousin were further molested in the private exercise of her religion. Since it was obvious that she could not be bullied into yielding and would positively welcome prosecution, John Dudley switched his attack. In April 1551 one of her chaplains was arrested for saying Mass, and in August her Comptroller and two other senior members of her household were also taken into custody for aiding and abetting their mistress in her defiance of the law. In a burst of temper, Mary told a government commission which visited her at the end of the month that, in the absence of her Comptroller, she was now obliged to do her own accounts and 'learn how many loaves of bread be made of a bushel of wheat'; but since her mother and father had not brought her up to baking and brewing, she would be glad to have him back. At the same time she flatly refused to accept the replacement offered by the Council. She would continue to appoint her own officers, and if anyone was forced upon her, she would go out of her gates, 'for they two should not dwell in one house'. When Nicholas Ridley, the new Bishop of London, reproached her for refusing to listen to God's word, she retorted: 'I cannot tell what ye call God's word; that is not God's word now, that was God's word in my father's days.' 'God's word', replied the Bishop unwisely, 'is one in all times; but hath been better understood and practised in some ages than others.' This was too much for Mary. 'You durst not, for your ears,' she cried, 'have avouched that for God's word in my father's days that now you do. And as for your new books, I thank God I never read any of them. I never did, nor ever will do.'

But although the Princess usually had the last word in such encounters, the Council had won the battle. Her household had been manœuvred into submission, and for the next two years, if their mistress heard Mass, it was in fear and secrecy behind locked doors. This was the second time in her life that Mary had been defeated on a matter of principle, but at least she had gone down fighting, making it abundantly clear that she had only surrendered to superior force. No one could be in any doubt about the strength of her convictions, nor of what her attitude would be were she ever to succeed to the throne.

By the early spring of 1553 this had become a matter of acute concern, for those in power could no longer conceal from themselves that Edward was mortally ill. The previous summer the young King had unfortunately succumbed to a sharp attack of measles, and now tuberculosis, which had already carried off three promising teenage Tudor boys, was taking its inevitable course. To John Dudley, Duke of Northumberland, that brilliant, unscrupulous soldier of fortune who had risen to power by ruthlessly exploiting the weaknesses of the late Lord Protector and who dominated the other members of the Council of Regency by the most hypnotic force of his personality, Edward's death threatened personal disaster. But the Duke did not intend to relinquish pride of place if he could help it, and he spent the spring and summer of 1553 working desperately to secure the future. His plan was a simple one. The King, like his father, would dispose of the Crown by Will, disinheriting both his half-sisters in favour of his cousin Jane Grey and, to ensure continued Dudley ascendancy, Jane would be married forthwith to Guildford, the youngest of Northumberland's brood of sons, who was fortunately still a bachelor.

Despite the barefaced illegality of the scheme, Edward needed little persuading to fall in with it. Wholly committed to the new religion, he was as anxious as Duke Dudley to exclude Mary, knowing that she would strive to bring back the idolatry of the Mass and undo all the godly work of the past five years. The same objection could not be urged against Elizabeth but, as Northumberland pointed out, it would be difficult to pass over one princess and not the other. In any case, both had been declared bastards by Act of Parliament and both might marry foreign princes, who would take control of the government 'to the utter subversion of the commonwealth'. Equally important, Elizabeth would be no more amenable than Mary to Dudley control. Jane Grey, on the other hand, was still only fifteen; she had been strictly brought up and would do as she was told. Her parents, too, could be relied on to play their part. The Dorsets – or the Suffolks as they now were, since her late father's dukedom had devolved upon Frances Brandon – had been disappointed of seeing their daughter married to the King; the prospect of seeing her become a Queen in her own right was guaranteed to entrance them.

After the arrest of Thomas Seymour, Jane had gone back to live at home, but her relations with her mother and father had not improved. She told Roger Ascham –

When I am in presence of either father or mother, whether I speak, keep silence, sit, stand or go, eat, drink, be merry or sad, be sewing, playing, dancing or doing anything else, I must do it ... even as perfectly as God made the world – or else I am so sharply taunted, so cruelly threatened, yea, presented sometimes with pinches, nips and bobs [blows] and other ways – which I will not name for the honour I bear them – so without measure misordered, that I think myself in hell.

Not surprisingly, Jane sought solace in her studies under the sympathetic guidance of her tutor, John Aylmer. When Ascham visited the family at Bradgate, their Leicestershire estate, in the winter, of 1550, he found her deep in Plato's *Phaedo*, reading it 'with as much delight as if it had been a merry tale of Boccaccio'. At fourteen she was conducting a learned correspondence (in Latin, naturally) with a group of Calvinist divines in Switzerland and seeking their advice on the pursuance of her Hebrew studies, so that she could read the Old Testament in the original.

Jane's only escape from the tyranny of her parents would, of course, be through marriage, but when Guildford Dudley was presented to her as her future husband, she refused him – or tried to do so. She seems to have disliked and feared all the Dudleys – feelings which many people shared – and besides, she considered herself to be already contracted to the Earl of

Hertford, son of the former Protector. Her resistance, though, was useless. According to a contemporary Italian account, her parents fell on her with blows and curses, and the wedding duly took place amid much pomp and ceremony on 25 May 1553.

The marriage of Jane Grey to Guildford Dudley remains the most famous example in Tudor times of a reluctant bride forced to the altar by an ambitious or mercenary family; but how often a similar fate overtook other, less important, less well-documented young ladies, is difficult to say. Certainly forced marriages were frowned upon by society at large. The Church insisted on the 'full and free consent' of both parties as an essential pre-condition for entering into the holy estate, and all writers on the subject were of the same opinion. Parents and guardians grievously offended by compelling their sons and daughters to be married to such as they hated, without any consideration of age, love, condition and manners, declared Henry Cornelius Agrippa in his *Commendation of Matrimony*. Another authority described forced marriage as 'the extremest bondage there is'. While yet another, Thomas Heywood, made the point that such marriages were bound to be self-defeating. 'How often', he enquired, 'have forced contracts been made to add land to land, not love to love? And to unite houses to houses, not hearts to hearts? which hath been the occasion that men have turned monsters, and women devils.'

Fulminations of this kind show that forced contracts were by no means unknown but, at the same time, it's probably fair to assume that they were uncommon. Not many parents were heartless enough to drive unwilling daughters into the arms of men they really detested or found physically repugnant and, although the concept of romantic love found little place in the normal run of sixteenth-century marriage negotiations, it was generally accepted that there should be 'liking' and a reasonable amount of compatibility between an engaged couple. In any case, sensible parents – and the majority of parents were sensible people – could see the force of Thomas Heywood's warning. An unhappy, discontented wife could quickly poison not only her husband's life but her in-laws' as well. The quarrels of an unhappy, ill-matched couple would inevitably spill over on to their respective families, sides would be taken and bad feeling spread through the small, tightly-knit community of town or village.

Some parents were more enlightened than others in this respect. The Dowager Duchess of Suffolk, when discussing the possibility of a marriage between one of her sons and the Duke of Somerset's daughter, had been very reluctant to bind the children to an engagement before they were old enough to judge the matter for themselves. She personally was all in favour of the alliance but, she wrote, 'no unadvised bonds between a boy and girl can give such assurance of good will, as hath been tried already'. 'I cannot tell', she went on, 'what more unkindness one of us might show the other, or wherein we might work more wickedly, than to bring our children into so miserable a state, as not to choose by their own liking such as they must profess so strait a bond, and so great a love to, for ever.' As the Duchess pointed out, once they realized they had married only to please their parents, or out of obedience, and had lost their 'free choice', neither of them would 'think themselves so much bounden to the other, a fault sufficient to break the greatest love'. If, later on, the young people were to 'make up the matter themselves', well and good. If not, then 'neither they nor one of us shall blame another'. As it happened, the matter never was made up, for the bridegroom elect died of the sweating sickness while still in his teens.

In practice, sons could expect to exercise fuller and freer consent than daughters. Trained from earliest childhood to obedience and passivity, to believing that her parents knew best, it took considerable courage and strength of will on the part of any well-brought-up girl to withstand family pressure in the matter of her marriage – and family pressure did not have to include physical violence to be compelling. Even the best-brought-up girl had a right to object if her father was proposing a dishonourable or unequal marriage – if, for example, the bridegroom were noticeably beneath her in social status or so much older that he would be unlikely to be able to give her children; but to reject an otherwise eligible suitor on the grounds that he was a bore, picked his nose or laughed at his own jokes, would be considered perverse and ungrateful by even the most indulgent father. So very many young women – especially those without a great deal to offer in the way of beauty or dowry – resigned themselves to accepting their parents' choice and prepared to make the best of it, hoping their mothers were right in their earnest assurances that love would follow marriage.

There were love matches too, of course. No one had anything against love, providing the price was right, and plenty of youthful romances flourished with parental approval. The great Duke of Northumberland himself had allowed his son Robert to marry for love, although the fate of that particular marriage rather justified those spoil-sports who maintained that a union founded on carnal love alone all too often ended in sorrow.

King Edward had been a guest at the wedding of Robert Dudley and Amye Robsart in June 1550, but he did not grace the marriage of Lady Jane Grey and Guildford Dudley. In May 1553 Edward was nearing the end of his sufferings, while alone in the country Mary waited in 'sore perplexity' and increasing fear of the future. Northumberland had become more conciliatory towards her in recent months, sending her bulletins on the King's condition, and when she last visited London in February had received her with greater courtesy than on previous occasions. But Mary was not deceived. She knew the Duke to be her enemy who would destroy her if he could, but as long as Edward lived, there was nothing to be done but wait.

Towards the end of the first week in July, both Mary and Elizabeth received urgent summonses to their brother's bedside. Elizabeth promptly took to her bed – too ill to travel, she declared, and ready with a doctor's certificate to prove it. Mary, then at Hunsdon, set out hesitantly on the journey but got no further than Hoddesdon on the London road before she was met by an anonymous messenger, a goldsmith of the City says one account, who told her that Edward was already dead and Northumberland's summons a trap. Pausing only to send a hasty word to the Imperial embassy, Mary turned aside and, accompanied only by two ladies and six loyal gentlemen of the household, made for her manor of Kenninghall in Norfolk. She had friends in the eastern counties, and there, if the worst happened, she would be well placed for flight to the Low Countries and sanctuary.

As Mary and her little party pushed on down the road which ran straight for mile after mile through the flat fertile farmlands of East Anglia, she probably had no very clear plans in mind. She was too much of a Tudor, and too much her mother's daughter, to be ready to give in without a fight, but she can have had few illusions about the desperate nature of her predicament. Certainly few outsiders believed she had a chance. She might be King Harry's daughter and the rightful heir, but Northumberland was the man in power. With the Council in his pocket, he controlled the capital, the treasury, the navy, the fortress of the Tower and its armoury, and had the reputation of being 'the best man of war' in the realm. Opposing him was a frail, sickly woman in her late thirties, without money, soldiers, advice or any organized support. The result of such a contest looked to be a foregone conclusion. But the Duke knew how narrow his power base really was and how quickly most of his supporters would desert him the moment the going got rough. His survival depended on a swift, bloodless success, and every day that Mary remained at large shortened the odds in her favour.

By Sunday, 9 July, she had reached the comparative safety of Kenninghall, and Northumberland had been forced to show his hand. The Bishop of London, preaching at St Paul's Cross, attacked both the Princesses as bastards but especially Mary, a papist who would bring foreigners into the country. On the following day Jane Grey was proclaimed Queen and brought in stately procession to the Tower, her Dudley husband, resplendent in white and gold, preening himself at her side and her mother acting as her train-bearer. But that evening, just as the new Court was sitting down to dinner, a letter arrived from the rival Queen defiantly ordering the Lords of the Council to proclaim *her* right and title in her city of London. Still no one really believed she stood a chance, but clearly she'd evaded the party of three hundred horse sent out with orders to catch and take her prisoner, and hopes of a swift, bloodless success were receding.

In fact, for Mary, the miracle was already happening. She hadn't stayed long at Kenninghall and by 11 July was established at Framlingham Castle, a fortified place closer to the sea. She may still have been considering the possibility of flight, but now every day that passed was making the necessity for that last, humiliating admission of defeat seem less urgent. Even before she left Kenninghall, substantial local gentlemen like Sir Henry Bedingfield and Harry Jerningham had rallied to her with their tenantry, and at Framlingham, where she raised her standard for the first time, more and more volunteers were coming to offer their allegiance. Important men like Sir Thomas Wharton, Sir John Mordaunt, Sir Edward Hastings, the Earl of Sussex and his son, and the Earl of Bath were on their way to join her, while 'innumerable small companies of the common people' carrying their makeshift weapons, trudged through the lanes towards the castle in a spontaneous, heartwarming show of support for the true Tudor line. On 12 July the town of Norwich had her publicly proclaimed and sent her men and supplies, and on the fourteenth the crews of the royal ships lying off Yarmouth came over to her in a body, bringing their captains and their heavy guns with them. This was such an encouraging development that Mary decided the time had come to review her forces; but as she rode along the ranks the enthusiasm was so great, the cries of 'Long live our good Queen Mary!' and the firing-off of harquebuses so deafening that her palfrey, who was used to a quiet life, would do nothing but rear. So the Queen had to dismount and go about the camp on foot, her eyes filling with ready tears at the sight of so much loyalty and true devotion.

Meanwhile, the Duke of Northumberland had ridden out of London at the head of a hastily-mustered army, which was being paid at the unusually high rate of tenpence a day, with the avowed aim of fetching in the Lady Mary like the rebel she was. But the good fortune, sense of timing and genius for command which had always combined to sustain him in the past, were no longer there. His men began to melt away, and the reinforcements he had been promised did not materialize. Herded together in the Tower, his confederates, having manœuvred him into the exposed position of field commander, were already planning to disown him, and the news now coming in of Mary's growing strength panicked them into action. On 18 July the decision was taken, and between five and six o'clock on the following afternoon the Council proclaimed Mary Tudor 'Queen of England, France and Ireland, and all dominions, as the sister of the late King Edward vi and daughter unto the noble King Henry viii'. Popular reaction was unmistakable. 'The bonfires were without number,' reported an anonymous correspondent in the City, 'and what with shouting and crying of the people, and ringing of the bells, there could no one hear almost what another said, besides banquetings and singing in the streets for joy.'

Even in Protestant London, relief at the downfall of Northumberland and the failure of his attempted *coup* more than outweighed the fact of Mary's Catholicism – for the present at least. But no one out on the streets that summer night, singing and feasting and drinking Queen Mary's health, was thinking much about the future, or about the likely fate of the fifteen-year-old girl who had reigned for nine days as Queen. Faint echoes of the general rejoicing could be heard in the Tower where, so it was said, the Duke of Suffolk had broken the news to his daughter and with his own hands helped to tear down the cloth of estate above her head, saying such things were not for her. Then he had gone out on to Tower Hill and proclaimed the Lady Mary's Grace to be Queen of England, before scuttling away to his house at Sheen. Jane was left alone, a prisoner in the stripped and silent rooms which a few hours before had been her palace – for her there would be no going home.

The new Queen was now making her way slowly and still cautiously towards the capital. By the end of July she had reached the village of Wanstead, and there she was greeted by the Princess Elizabeth, apparently quite recovered from her recent illness, who had ridden out accompanied by a numerous train of gentlemen, knights and ladies to escort her sister on the last stage of her journey. It was some years since the two had met, but the reunion seemed an affectionate one, and Mary gave Elizabeth a prominent place in the procession which, on the evening of 3 August, entered the City at Aldgate to pass through streets decorated with banners and streamers and lined with wildly cheering crowds.

They made a painful contrast, these two daughters of Henry VIII. Mary had once been a pretty, graceful girl, with an exceptionally beautiful complexion. Dispassionate observers could still describe her as 'fresh-coloured', but the long years of unhappiness, ill-health and unkindness had left their mark, and at thirty-seven the Queen was a thin, sandy-haired, tight-lipped little woman who looked her age and more. Elizabeth, riding less than a horse's length behind her, would be twenty in a month's time. She was never considered a beauty, 'comely rather than handsome', remarked the Venetian ambassador, but she had grown into a tall, elegant young woman with a clear, pale skin and the family's reddish-gold hair who, like her mother, knew how to make the best of herself. She held herself well, dressed with a severe simplicity which suited her admirably and had beautiful hands which she took care to display. More important, she was young, Protestant and Tudor, and there can be little doubt that to very many of the citizens of London it was Elizabeth who represented their hopes for the future.

While her first, brief incredulous flush of happiness lasted, Mary showed her sister a marked degree of attention, holding her by the hand whenever they appeared in public together and always giving her the place of honour at her side – a cosy state of affairs which lasted no longer than a matter of weeks. Mary, to her credit, had never borne malice to the child Elizabeth, who'd once been the innocent cause of so much jealous misery, but the adult Elizabeth was quite a different proposition, and Catherine of Aragon's daughter was finding it increasingly difficult to conceal her instinctive dislike of the cool, self-possessed young lady whose presence served as a constant reminder of that infamous woman, Nan Bullen the whore.

The immediate bone of contention was, inevitably, religion. Mary never doubted for one moment that her miraculous preservation had been due entirely to the personal intervention of the Almighty, or that it was now her clear and sacred duty to lead her people back into the fold of the true Church, and Mass, though still officially illegal, was already being publicly celebrated at Court. The Lords of the Council, with the embarrassment of recent events fresh in their minds, attended assiduously, but the Princess Elizabeth did not put in an appearance until the beginning of September and even then contrived to make it pretty plain that she was doing so under duress.

The burgeoning hostility between the Queen and her heiress presumptive was also, unfortunately, receiving outside encouragement. Mary, accustomed since her teens to relying on her mother's family for guidance and support, was now turning to Simon Renard, the new Imperial ambassador, as naturally and trustfully as in the past she had turned to Eustace Chapuys; and Renard, a shrewd and skilful diplomat whose task was to rebuild the Anglo-Imperial alliance, regarded the heretical Elizabeth as a serious potential danger – an obvious focal point for domestic discontent, whether religious or political. He told the Emperor, in a curiously felicitous phrase, that she had 'a spirit full of enchantment' and was greatly to be feared. He told the Queen, frequently and unnecessarily, not to trust her sister, as she was 'clever and sly' and might easily prove disloyal. The French, too, had an interest in promoting dissension at the English Court. The young Queen of Scotland would soon be ready for her long-planned marriage with the Dauphin and, despite the provisions of her great-uncle Henry's Will, she still possessed, by all the accepted laws of inheritance, a strong claim to the reversion of the English crown. The King of France was naturally much attracted by the prospect of seeing his daughter-in-law become queen of both the island kingdoms, and if the Tudor sisters could be provoked or tricked into destroying one another, he was by no means unhopeful of the issue.

Certainly relations between the Tudor sisters seemed to be going from bad to worse. Mary did not believe Elizabeth's assurances that she went to Mass 'because her conscience prompted and moved her to it', and in a hysterical outburst that autumn she cried out that it would be a scandal and a disgrace to the kingdom to allow her sister to succeed her, as she was a heretic, a hypocrite and a bastard. On another occasion the Queen went so far as to declare that she couldn't even be certain Elizabeth was King Henry's bastard, for she looked just like Mark Smeaton the lute-player, one of the young men who had died with Anne Boleyn.

Elizabeth managed to secure her proper place at Mary's coronation (she was paired in the procession with that old family friend, Anne of Cleves) but what with the Queen's undisguised rancour, Renard's unsleeping distrust and the false-friend approaches of the French ambassador, her position was becoming acutely uncomfortable, and she asked permission to retire from the Court. After some hesitation, permission was granted, and early in December the sisters met to say goodbye. Elizabeth once more protested her loyalty and good intentions, begging the Queen not to listen to 'evil reports' of her, while Mary, unusually gracious, responded with an expensive parting present of a sable hood. This apparent détente was largely the work of Simon Renard, who had explained patiently to the Queen that she must make up her mind either to treat Elizabeth as an enemy and put her under some form of restraint, or else, for reasons of policy, behave towards her with at least outward civility. Mary could not bring herself to adopt the first of these alternatives, but Renard reported that he'd had a good deal of difficulty in persuading her to dissemble. 'She still resents the injuries inflicted on Queen Catherine, her lady mother, by the machinations of Anne Boleyn, mother of Elizabeth,' he wrote with a hint of exasperation.

Mary had now been on the throne for nearly six months and was finding the exercise of power both harassing and uncongenial. A well-meaning woman of rigid moral principles – a simple, painfully honest woman, narrow in outlook and limited in experience – she was hopelessly out of her depth in the complicated, unprincipled world of high politics and possessed none of the toughness of mind essential for a successful working monarch. Not, of course, that anyone expected her to cope with this unfeminine task alone. Everyone took it for granted that she needed a husband to relieve her of the burden of government and undertake, as Simon Renard tactfully put it, 'those duties which were not the province of ladies'. But there was widespread disappointment and dismay when the Queen made it clear that she had no intention of choosing an English husband. Dismay turned to consternation when it became known that she intended to marry the Emperor's son, Philip of Spain, and people began to remind one another of the Duke of Northumberland's predictions that Mary would bring foreigners and papists into the country.

Opposition to the Spanish marriage hardened rapidly but the Queen clung to her purpose. The fact that Philip, a good-looking young man in his late twenties and heir to half the thrones of Europe, happened to be the most brilliant match available weighed far less with her than the fact that he was a Spaniard and of her mother's kin. Skilfully encouraged by Renard and driven by her own craving for the affection and security she had for so long been denied, Mary was already more than half in love – a heady sensation for one who had 'never harboured thoughts of voluptuousness' and had hitherto schooled herself to an almost nunlike renunciation of the flesh. She did not reach her decision lightly but when, after weeks of heart-searching and prayer, Mary gave her word to Renard in the presence of the Holy Sacrament, she had convinced herself that it was God's will for her to marry Philip, and after that she was immovable. She paid no attention to those friends and councillors who tried to warn her of the trouble she was storing up for herself. She huffily dismissed a parliamentary delegation which came to beg her to marry an Englishman, telling them they had no business to dictate to her on such a personal matter and anyway, if they forced her to marry against her will, she would not live three months, and then they would be sorry! Even more foolishly, she shut her ears to the ominous rumblings of popular alarm at the prospect of being ruled by 'the proud Spaniard'.

In fact, in drawing up the marriage treaty, the Emperor was leaning over backwards in his efforts not to offend the delicate susceptibilities of the English – an alliance which would give him command of the sea route between Spain and the Netherlands was worth any amount of diplomacy. But the English were currently in the grip of one of their periodic attacks of xenophobia, and many otherwise quite sensible people preferred to believe the rumours being spread by various interested parties, who included the French ambassador and the radical wing of the Protestant party, that a horde of Spaniards, all armed to the teeth, would shortly be landing on their coasts ready to ravish their wives, deflower their daughters and despoil them of their goods and lands; that England was about to become a province of the Empire and that the Pope's authority would be restored by force.

By the beginning of February 1554, this rising tide of panic and prejudice had erupted into the most serious revolt against the authority of the Crown within living memory, and Sir Thomas Wyatt and his Kentishmen came very close indeed to gaining control of the capital. That they failed was due in large part to Mary's own courage and her stubborn refusal to be intimidated by violence. Ignoring advice that she should seek her own safety, she went down to the City and made a fighting speech in the crowded Guildhall which not even Elizabeth could have bettered. Although her own presence chamber at Whitehall was full of armed men, the gentlemen pensioners with their pole-axes in their hands; although her ladies made 'great lamentations', weeping and wringing their hands; although at one point the sound of gunfire around Charing Cross could be heard within the precincts of the palace, the Queen stood fast – a gallant little figure watching from the gallery over the gatehouse, sending word that she would 'tarry to see the uttermost' and unmoved by the general terror and confusion, the slamming of doors and the 'running and shrieking of gentlewomen'.

The rebellion collapsed, but the Queen could now no longer afford the luxury of showing mercy to her enemies, and one of the first victims of the government's new hard-line policy was, tragically, Lady Jane Grey. Mary had so far refused to sanction her cousin's execution. Jane, she had told Renard the previous summer, was not to be blamed for Northumberland's treason. The child had been helpless in his grasp, and Mary's conscience would not allow her to see an innocent, if misguided, young creature put to death. Jane must stand trial and stay in the Tower for a while, but as soon as it seemed safe to do so, the Queen intended to set her free. In the aftermath of armed rebellion, things looked rather different. Innocent Jane might be, but this did not alter the fact that her very existence had come to represent an unacceptable danger to the state. Her own father's behaviour had made that only too clear, for the Duke of Suffolk, who owed his continued life and liberty entirely to Mary's generosity, had tried to raise the Midlands on his daughter's behalf. Jane had been named as heir by the late King Edward (who now wore a Protestant halo). She had been publicly proclaimed and had actually worn the crown. As long as she lived, she could be used again as the figure head for a Protestant plot. Few people urged this view more strongly than those lords of the Council, so recently prominent Protestant plotters themselves, who were now acutely anxious that this inconvenient reminder of their past indiscretions should be permanently removed. Mary would have saved Jane if it had been within her power, but neither Mary, for all her obstinate, conscientious courage, nor Jane, with her brilliant intellect, was a match for the desperate, ruthless men who surrounded them. Both in their different ways were the helpless victims of their circumstances.

Jane was beheaded on Tower Green on the morning of 12

February. The two ladies who attended her 'wonderfully wept', but she herself was dry-eyed and calm. In a brief speech from the scaffold, she admitted she had done wrong in ever accepting the crown but reiterated her innocency 'touching the procurement and desire thereof'. She asked those present to bear witness that she died a good Christian woman who looked to be saved 'by none other mean, but only by the mercy of God in the merits of the blood of His only son Jesus Christ'. 'And now, good people,' she ended, 'while I am alive, I pray you to assist me with your prayers.' Even at the last dreadful moment, she had the strength to remain true to her Protestant faith which rejected the age-old comfort of prayers for the dead. Jane had known little happiness in her sixteen years of life, but all her learning had taught her that earthly happiness was a vain and transient thing. She was going now to a better place, and that conviction sustained her. It was only after the blindfold had been tied over her eyes and she was alone and groping in the dark that her composure broke momentarily. Then someone came forward to guide her, and 'she laid her down upon the block and stretched forth her body and said: "Lord, into thy hands I commend my spirit."' Later that day the butchered remains of Henry VIII's eldest great-niece were thrust unceremoniously beneath the stones of St Peter-ad-Vincula, to lie between his two headless queens, Anne Boleyn and Katherine Howard.

No one denied that Jane Grey had been a sacrifice to political necessity, and for a time it looked as if another, still greater sacrifice would be exacted. Throughout the recent crisis the Princess Elizabeth had remained in the country, holed up at her house at Ashridge and suffering, so she assured the Queen, from such a cold and headache as she had never felt before. Elizabeth's name had never been publicly invoked by Wyatt, but it was an open secret that the rebels' ultimate aim had been to depose the Queen, marry Elizabeth to young Edward Courtenay, great-grandson of Edward IV and last male offshoot of the Plantagenet tree, and place them jointly on the throne. Certainly this was what the French ambassador, in his anxiety to prevent the Spanish marriage at all costs, had been hoping to see. There was no evidence as yet that Elizabeth had been in contact with Wyatt, or had known or approved of his plans, but there were one or two suspicious circumstances, and there could be no doubt that she, if anyone, had stood to gain by his success. She was therefore brought under guard to London to give an account of herself, despite her pleas that her weakness was so great that she feared she would not be able to endure the journey without peril of life.

Her illness on this occasion was genuine enough, but the danger, as she well knew, lay not in the journey but its destination. How great that danger might be must surely have been brought home by the news of Jane Grey's execution. For if Mary had been able to bring herself to kill Jane, who'd always been rather a favourite with her, what chance was there that she would spare the sister she so openly distrusted? As it turned out, it was Mary's scrupulous insistence on a thorough and careful investigation of all the facts, that and her own impenetrable discretion, which saved Elizabeth. Her much publicized sojourn in the Tower was undoubtedly a frightening and upsetting experience, but by the time the hotly-debated decision to send her there had been taken, it was already becoming clear that no proof of treasonable intent was likely to be forthcoming. Elizabeth herself denied everything, and since she had written no letters, had apparently given no promises or encouragement to the conspirators – at any rate none of the other prisoners could be induced to accuse her – the enquiry seemed to have reached a dead end.

A trifling detail such as lack of evidence might not have mattered in the days of Henry VIII, but Mary possessed none of her father's ruthless self-confidence. Even now, to Simon Renard's barely suppressed annoyance, she was beginning to pardon her rebels, and he thought it would not be long before she was persuaded to release her sister. Mary's opinion of Elizabeth had not changed; she still believed her to be without conscience, dishonest, deceitful and most probably disloyal. All the same, in spite of her personal dislike of the girl, and in spite of Renard's hints that he hardly dared advise Prince Philip to hazard his precious person in a country which continued to harbour so dangerous a character as Elizabeth Tudor, the Queen stuck grimly to her principles. As long as the case against her remained unproven, Elizabeth would continue to get the benefit of the doubt, and by the middle of May the Princess, demurely inscrutable as ever, had left her prison quarters to spend an indefinite period of house arrest at the old royal hunting-lodge at Woodstock, in the custody of Sir Henry Bedingfield, one of those sturdy Catholic gentlemen who had come to Mary's aid the previous summer.

Mary herself was sick of London, where violent demonstrations against her religion, her policies and her marriage were once more appearing on the streets, and where she seemed to spend her days struggling with a refractory and quarrelsome Council, few of whose members she trusted further than she could see them. So, at the end of the month, she thankfully shook the dust of the insolent, heretical city and moved out to Richmond on the first stage of her journey to Winchester, where Philip was to join her. Philip himself, having delayed as long, or rather longer than he decently could, finally landed at Southampton at the end of July, and the blood-stained monster of the Protestant propaganda machine was discovered to be a slim, dapper young man, slightly below average height, whose blue eyes and yellow hair gave him a reassuringly un-foreign appearance.

The betrothed couple met for the first time informally in the long gallery of the bishop's palace and sat together talking in a mixture of Spanish and French, for Philip had not considered it necessary to learn any English. The following day he came to see the Queen again, and they had another brief private talk, 'each of them merrily smiling on the other, to the great comfort and joy of the beholders'. No one was in any doubt what the Queen thought of Philip, and she was already beginning to shower him with expensive presents. Philip, though unfailingly polite and attentive to his bride, kept his thoughts to himself, but the other Spaniards, in their letters home, were less discreet.

The Queen was a dear, good creature and a perfect saint, but older than they'd been led to suppose and had no idea how to dress. She was certainly not beautiful and had no eyebrows, but she might perhaps look better and less flabby if she could be persuaded to adopt Spanish fashions. Philip's friend Ruy Gomez thought it was just as well the Prince understood his marriage had been arranged for political and not fleshly considerations, for this elderly, faded virgin would obviously be no good in bed.

The wedding took place in Winchester Cathedral on Wednesday, 25 July. The Queen was given away on behalf of the nation by a posse of noblemen headed by the old Marquess of Winchester, and the ceremony was conducted with all the solemn ritual, all the pomp and splendour, proper to the marriage of a reigning queen; but Mary's wedding ring was, at her own insistence, a plain gold band, 'because maidens were so married in old times'. Throughout the hour-long nuptial Mass she remained motionless, her eyes fixed on the sacrament, wrapt in a trance of happiness and luxuriating in the knowledge that she was no longer alone, no longer a despised old maid. With Philip at her side, the heretics and traitors who surrounded her would become powerless, and she would know the unutterable joy of seeing the holy Mother Church restored, free at last of that burden of guilt she had carried for nearly twenty years. To Mary in that moment God seemed very good.

After the service, the Queen and her husband walked hand-in-hand back to the bishop's palace for a sumptuous wedding breakfast, eaten off gold plate, with the musicians playing and heralds crying largesse. Later there was dancing, and finally, after a quiet supper in their private apartments, the Bishop of Winchester blessed the marriage bed, and the bridal couple were left alone. 'What happened that night', wrote one of Philip's Spaniards, 'only they know, but if they give us a son our joy will be complete.' And well it might be, at least from the Emperor's point of view. It was on the hope of a son that the alliance had been founded, for with a half-Hapsburg king on the English throne, the Imperial family would have absorbed the wealthy and strategic island as easily and cheaply as in the previous generation they had absorbed Spain, and the rich Burgundian inheritance of the Netherlands in the generation before that.

CHAPTER EIGHT

But One Mistress and No Master

The autumn and winter of 1554 was probably the happiest time of Mary's adult life. Now that her marriage had become an accomplished fact, most people seemed ready to accept it, and, although relations between the Londoners and Philip's Spaniards were never less than strained, organized hostility was confined to isolated incidents. The Court was very gay, the Queen was reported to be looking fatter and a better colour, and soon she announced herself to be pregnant. That autumn, too, Parliament, its members carefully chosen from 'the wise, grave and Catholic sort', completed the work of undoing the Reformation, abrogating Royal Supremacy and restoring all the ancient laws and penalties against heresy. By November the reconciliation with Rome had been achieved, and Cardinal Pole, the first papal legate to set foot in England since the far-off days of the King's 'great matter', came to Westminster bringing the Pope's absolution for the schismatic islanders. It was an especially poignant moment for Mary, for Reginald Pole was a kinsman of hers, son of Margaret Countess of Salisbury, once her governess and close friend – 'a lady of virtue and honour if ever there was one in England' – executed by Henry VIII in the purge of the late thirties. The Cardinal brought memories of happy childhood days as well as tangible evidence of the fulfilment of hope, and as she greeted him the Queen felt joyfully convinced that 'the babe had quickened and leapt in her womb'.

The New Year came in and by March preparations for the royal confinement were under way. Early in April Mary moved to Hampton Court, ready to 'take her chamber', and by the middle of the month the midwives, nurses and rockers were in attendance and the palace was crowded with noble ladies come to support the Queen through her ordeal. By the end of the month there was another noble lady at Hampton Court whose presence gave the Queen little comfort, for, at Philip's insistence, Elizabeth had been brought up from Woodstock and reluctantly 'forgiven' by her sister.

The King had been taking out some personal insurance by arranging that the heir presumptive should be at hand during his wife's lying-in. If Mary were to die in childbed, he would, after all, be very much alone in hostile territory and might find it useful to have a hostage, or perhaps an ally. But he was also thinking further ahead. If, as was quite possible, the Queen failed to produce a living child, Elizabeth's right to succeed would have to be supported by Spain. Heretic, hypocrite and bastard though she might be, she would still be an infinitely preferable alternative to the French-controlled Queen of Scotland. Philip and his advisers had therefore come round to the idea that it would be sensible to establish friendly relations with the Princess at a time when she would be grateful for her brother-in-law's good offices, and while she was still young enough to be influenced. A suitable imperialist husband could then be found for her, and the future of the alliance would be assured. The Princess herself was more than willing to be friends, and it was noticed that 'at the time of the Queen's pregnancy, the Lady Elizabeth ... contrived so to ingratiate herself with all the Spaniards, and especially with the King, that ever since no one has favoured her more than he does'.

The Lady Elizabeth, of course, was taking out some insurance on her own account, for this was an anxious time for the heir to the throne. Few people, remembering her mother's misfortunes and considering the poor state of Mary's health, which had never recovered from the strain and misery she had endured at the time of her parents' divorce, seriously thought she could now bear a healthy child. But if she did – and Mary had already once triumphed against seemingly impossible odds

– then Elizabeth's prospects would vanish overnight and the English political scene would be transformed, perhaps for generations to come. As Simon Renard observed, 'everything in this kingdom depends on the Queen's safe deliverance'.

Meanwhile, everything possible was being done to encourage the Queen. The Venetian ambassador reported on 24 April that to comfort her and give her heart and courage, 'three most beautiful infants were brought for her Majesty to see; they having been born a few days previously at one birth, of a woman of low stature and great age like the Queen, who after delivery found herself strong and out of danger'. Those who believed the pregnancy to be a myth, or a Spanish trick, or that 'it was only a tumour, as often happens to women', were keeping their mouths shut – at least for the time being.

At daybreak on 30 April a rumour reached London that Mary had given birth to a son just after midnight, 'with little pain and no danger'. So circumstantial was this report that it was generally believed, and since, whatever its implications, the birth of a prince was automatically an occasion for rejoicing, the church bells were rung and the citizens shut up shop and surged into the streets to light bonfires and drink the baby's health. It was late afternoon before the messengers returning from Hampton Court brought the news that there was no prince and no sign even that the birth was imminent. As the days of waiting lengthened into weeks, the doctors announced that their calculations had been wrong and that the Queen would not now be delivered until the end of May, possibly not until the beginning of June, although her Majesty's belly had greatly declined, an indication, it was said, of the nearer approach of the term. On 24 June, Renard reported that the Queen's doctors were two months out in their calculations, and she would not be delivered for another eight or ten days.

June turned into July, and still the empty cradle waited. But Mary refused to give up hope, and Sir John Mason in Brussels was ordered to contradict the now widespread gossip that the Queen was not pregnant at all and to assure the Emperor that she was near her time. The doctors and midwives continued to talk about miscalculation and to assure the wretched Queen that she was carrying a child, but hinting that she might not be delivered until August or even September. By this time, though, everyone knew there was no baby. The amenorrhoea and digestive troubles to which Mary had always been subject, and very likely incipient cancer of the womb, had combined with her desperate yearning (which, according to the omniscient Venetians, had even produced 'swelling of the paps and their emission of milk') to create that pathetic self-delusion.

Gossip was growing more and more unkind, and something had to be done to put an end to an acutely embarrassing situation – apart from anything else, the Queen's long seclusion and her refusal to attend to business was bringing the work of government to a virtual halt. So, on 3 August, a reduced household moved away to Oatlands on the pretext that Hampton Court needed cleansing, as indeed it must after four months' crowded occupation. The daily prayers and processions for the Queen's delivery were stopped, and Mary returned painfully to her normal routine, having suffered perhaps the most appalling disappointment and humiliation that any woman could experience. As if that were not enough, she now had to face the bitter fact that her adored husband was planning to leave her. Philip had spent more than a year in a country he disliked, being polite to people he despised and putting up with a good deal of dumb insolence in return. He felt he had done all that could reasonably be expected of him and, since his wife was obviously barren, there was nothing to be gained by staying. He sailed for the Netherlands at the end of the month, but before he went he took the precaution of recommending the Princess Elizabeth to the Queen's goodwill, following this up with written instructions that she was to be treated with every consideration.

Elizabeth was still at Court, and Mary, like an obedient wife, tried hard to conceal her 'evil disposition' towards Anne Boleyn's daughter under a mask of synthetic amiability, only conversing with her about 'agreeable subjects'. Elizabeth, too, was on her best behaviour, but the atmosphere remained thick with strain and mutual animosity, and as soon as she decently could, the Princess asked leave to go home. Back at Hatfield, the house always most closely associated with her early days, she settled down to wait, reasonably confident now about the future.

The last three years of Mary's life were for the Queen years of increasing ill-health, unhappiness and disillusion. For the country at large it was a time of economic depression and political unrest, darkened by the religious persecution which still shadows Mary's memory. The first heretics had gone to the stake in February 1555, and in all some three hundred people, including sixty women, were burned alive. It was not, by contemporary standards, an especially harsh campaign, but it lingers in the mind as a sad and nasty episode – one of its least attractive features being the fact that the great majority of the victims were humble people. The 'better sort' of Protestants either conformed just sufficiently to satisfy the authorities' not very exacting standards or else took themselves and their tender consciences abroad with very little hindrance. Among those who sought sanctuary in Protestant Switzerland or Germany was that outspoken radical Katherine, Duchess of Suffolk, and her second husband, young Mr Richard Bertie.

As head of state, Mary must, of course, bear final responsibility for the acts committed in her name, but to what extent she personally initiated the persecution which earned her her unenviable nickname remains in some doubt. In many ways she was the most merciful of the Tudors – certainly her leniency towards her political enemies bordered on recklessness – but while the Queen found it only too easy to forgive treason against herself, heresy was treason against God, and that was a different matter. Besides, the heretics were not only imperilling their immortal souls, they were infecting and endangering others by their example. To Mary it would have been an unthinkable dereliction of that duty which had been so clearly laid upon her, if she had not tried by every means at her disposal to save her miserable subjects from themselves.

From the point of view of what she was hoping to achieve,

her policy was a total failure. The fires which consumed the Protestant bishops Hooper, Latimer and Ridley, who, with Thomas Cranmer, were virtually the only sufferers of note, did indeed light such a candle in England as, with God's grace, never was put out. In the political climate of the time, Catholicism was becoming ineradicably associated with foreign oppression, and the Marian persecution sowed the seeds of an implacable fear and hatred of Rome and all its works. The Queen, naturally enough, could only see that the forces of darkness were more powerful even than she had feared, and together with Cardinal Pole, a high-minded, middle-aged scholar who understood as little as the Queen that politics was the art of the possible, she squandered the last of her strength in a useless struggle against the tide of history.

The Cardinal's sympathetic support gave Mary a little comfort in her loneliness, but she pined for Philip, who sent only promises – promises which were repeatedly and cynically broken – in response to her anguished, self-abasing pleas that he should come back, not just because she loved and needed him but so that their marriage might be fruitful. The months since his departure lengthened into a year, and Mary could only rage and despair by turn as time passed and her stubborn, unquenchable hopes of bearing children were mocked by her husband's absence.

Then, at the end of March 1557, Philip did come back. It was for a brief visit only, with only one objective – to drag England into the everlasting Franco-Spanish feud, just as the more thoughtful opponents of the Spanish marriage had always predicted he would. By July he was gone and, knowing perhaps that she would never see him again, Mary went with him to Dover, down to the water's edge. Philip was too busy now, with the renewal of the war and all the business of taking over from his father (the old Emperor was retiring to spend his last days in a monastery), to have time to spare for English affairs, but one piece of unfinished business continued to nag at the back of his mind. The Princess Elizabeth, now rising twenty-four, was still unmarried, still unfettered to the Spanish interest. It should have been a simple matter, and yet, to Philip's annoyance, the Tudor sisters were proving surprisingly difficult to manipulate. Elizabeth was saying flatly that she had no intention of marrying anyone, which of course was nonsense, but she was in too strong a position now to be easily coerced; and Mary, usually so amenable to her husband's commands, had turned stubborn. Philip wanted the Queen to recognize Elizabeth as her heir without further delay and, at the same time, to arrange her marriage to the Duke of Savoy, a reliable pensioner of the Imperial family. He sent his confessor, Francisco de Fresnada, to explain to Mary how essential this was for the safety of the realm, for the future of the restored religion (despite Elizabeth's dutiful attendance at Mass, no one believed in the sincerity of her 'conversion') and to prevent her from making some quite unsuitable choice of her own. But de Fresnada came up against the blank wall of Mary's bitter, obsessive jealousy. The Venetians heard that he found the Queen 'utterly averse to giving the Lady Elizabeth any hope of the succession, obstinately maintaining that she was neither her sister nor the daughter of the Queen's father, King Henry. Nor would she hear of favouring her, as she was born of an infamous woman, who had so greatly outraged the Queen her mother and herself.'

Philip, to whom the old feuds of the Tudor family were a tiresome irrelevance, was profoundly irritated, but Mary, although miserable in the knowledge of his displeasure, refused to budge. A sad, sick woman, faced with the realization that her beloved husband was thinking only of a future in which she would have no share, she was being asked publicly to concede that Anne Boleyn and her daughter had won the battle. She would not do it, not even for Philip, not even for the Holy Catholic Church. Poor Mary, if only things had been different, how she would have enjoyed finding a husband for her sister, fussing endlessly over the details of her trousseau, giving her good advice and standing godmother to her first child. But while Mary Tudor had been called upon to bear many sorrows in the course of her life, many disappointments and humiliations, perhaps the one thing she could not have borne would have been to see Elizabeth make a successful marriage and have the babies Mary herself had craved with all the force of her starved and passionate nature.

Philip had not abandoned his plans for the Princess's future, but it looked as if they would have to be shelved until he had a moment to push the business through in person. Somehow that moment never arrived. By the following summer the Queen was obviously failing, and by the autumn the news was sufficiently grave to make the King send Count de Feria over to England in a last effort to make her see sense. But when he arrived, on 9 November, it was to find that Mary had already suffered her last defeat. Three days earlier the Council had gathered at her bedside and spoken to her 'with a view to persuading her to make certain declarations in favour of the Lady Elizabeth concerning the succession', and Mary had given in, too tired to struggle any longer. A deputation had hurried down to Hatfield with the news, and the Queen was left in peace. She was unconscious for long periods during those last weeks, but once, when she drifted to the surface and saw her ladies in tears, she is said to have comforted them by telling them what good dreams she had, seeing many little children singing and playing before her. Mary had always loved little children, had revelled in weddings and christenings and new clothes, taking a passionate interest in those small domestic matters which filled the lives of ordinary women. She was herself a very ordinary woman at heart, made to be a busy, devoted wife and mother, happily ruling the small kingdom of the home. In the great world where she had been forced to live she could only do what she believed to be her duty, what she believed to be right. She had done her best, and it had not been good enough.

The Queen died at six o'clock in the morning of 17 November 1558, and later that same day Reginald Pole, Cardinal Archbishop of Canterbury, lying ill in his palace just across the river at Lambeth, also slipped away, thus closing a chapter with unusual tidiness. There was little pretence of mourning. The church bells pealed and bonfires illuminated the streets, while the Londoners 'did eat, drink and make merry for the new Queen Elizabeth'.

But although everyone, or nearly everyone, rejoiced at the ending of an inept and unlucky reign, there were those who felt misgivings about the future. After their recent unfortunate experience of petticoat government, there were those who wondered rather uneasily if that uncompromising Scot, John Knox, could perhaps be right in his recent assertion that 'it was more than a monster in nature that a woman should reign and have empire above men'. The new Queen was young and healthy and, in the opinion of the great majority of her subjects, by far the most valuable service she could render them would be to marry without delay and bear sturdy sons to secure their own and their children's future. This, as the Speaker of the House of Commons was soon to assure her, 'was the single, the only, the all-comprehending prayer of all Englishmen'. The new Queen, however, showed no immediate disposition to gratify this very reasonable desire. On the contrary, she continued at every opportunity to reiterate her settled preference for the single life, much to the exasperation of the men around her who found all this coy talk about perpetual virginity thoroughly tiresome.

In the society in which she lived, Elizabeth's outspoken aversion to the holy estate of matrimony and her stubborn refusal to accept her natural role of wife and mother seemed both incomprehensible and more than a little shocking. As she herself once remarked: 'There is a strong idea in the world that a woman cannot live unless she is married, or at all events that if she refrains from marriage she does so for some bad reason.' That Elizabeth Tudor's innermost reason for refraining from marriage was rooted in childhood traumas seems at least a plausible theory. Had not her father killed her mother and her mother's cousin for causes perhaps only dimly understood and yet demonstrably connected with sexual guilt? It would surely not be surprising if a conviction that physical love, shame and violent death were inextricably connected had formed in her subconscious mind by the time she was eight years old – a conviction which could only have been strengthened by her own adolescent experience at the hands of Thomas Seymour. On a less speculative level, Elizabeth had seen marriage bring unhappiness and death to her good friend Katherine Parr and had watched the degrading misery of unrequited love ravage her sister, another reigning queen. Of one thing she could be certain – that to surrender to physical passion, to give herself to a man, to any man, would diminish if not destroy her power both as a woman and as a queen, and Elizabeth lived and throve on the exercise of power. Within a month of her accession it was noted that she seemed 'incomparably more feared than her sister, and gives her orders and has her way as absolutely as her father did'.

Elizabeth was, of course, a phenomenon by the standards of any age. 'Her intellect and understanding are wonderful,' wrote the Venetian ambassador in the year before she came to the throne, and he went on to praise her ability as a linguist. Latin, still the universal language of diplomacy and culture, came as naturally to her as breathing. Her Italian was fluent, and she had 'no slight knowledge of Greek'. In the midst of all her other preoccupations, the Queen kept up her studies, reading with her old tutor Roger Ascham, who said of her during the early sixties: 'I believe that, besides her perfect readiness in Latin, Italian, French and Spanish, she readeth here now at Windsor more Greek every day than some prebendary of this church doth read Latin in a whole week.' Elizabeth maintained this habit of daily study throughout her life, and her capacity for sheer concentrated hard work was always immense.

No one who ever had anything to do with her could doubt the quality of her trained and formidable intelligence, but from the first weeks of her reign she also demonstrated that she possessed the precious attribute of personal magnetism. 'If ever any person had either the gift or the style to win the hearts of people, it was this Queen,' wrote the historian John Hayward, and Elizabeth's continuing love-affair with her subjects remains one of the wonders of the age. It was certainly one of her greatest sources of strength.

She was a born ruler and above all a born politician, shrewd, cautious and subtle. In circumstances where Mary had floundered unhappily, Elizabeth moved sure-footed and confident. Instead of meekly accepting her sex as an inescapable infirmity in a male-dominated world, she used it brilliantly and deliberately as a weapon in her life-long battle to avoid domination. Her private resolve to stay single did not for a moment prevent her from zestfully exploiting the advantages attached to being 'the best match in her parish', and for twenty years the Queen's various marriage projects provided her with an invaluable card in the diplomatic poker game. Her subjects would, of course, have preferred her to marry an Englishman but, fortunately for Elizabeth, there was no Englishman available of sufficiently high rank to make him acceptable to his peers. If Edward Courtenay had been still alive, even she might have found it impossible to resist the pressure which would have been brought to bear on her, but Edward Courtenay had died of fever in 1556, and there was no one else. Abroad, virtually every suitable prince was a Catholic, and the Queen at least knew very well that to attempt to introduce another Catholic consort into what had once more become a Protestant country would be asking for trouble of the most lurid kind – especially as the ideological warfare between the two creeds grew fiercer. But since nobody, not even those closest to her, could ever be quite certain what the Queen meant to do (the Queen, always a consummate actress, took care that they should not), negotiations with foreign powers were conducted with every appearance of serious intent and prolonged until they had served their purpose.

While she enjoyed being sought after as much as the next woman, the Queen's famous courtships were political ploys first and last. She found her friends nearer home. Elizabeth was no sexual deviant, at any rate not in any obvious sense. She never lost her eye for an attractive man and enjoyed male company, so long as it was on her own terms. Her obvious preference for the company of Robert Dudley was a cause of acute concern in the early years of the reign, and many people were seriously worried that the Queen might be wasting her time and spoiling her chances by having an affair with a married man. When Robert's wife died in mysterious circumstances, fear that she meant to throw herself away in a demeaning and disastrous marriage reached panic proportions in some quarters.

I wish I were either dead or hence [wrote Nicholas Throckmorton, English ambassador in Paris], that I might not hear the dishonourable and naughty reports that are made of the Queen.... One laugheth at us, another threateneth, another revileth the Queen. Some let not to say: What religion is this that a subject shall kill his wife and the Prince not only bear withal but marry with him? If these slanderous bruits be not slaked, or if they prove true, our reputation is gone forever, war follows and utter subversion of the Queen and country.

There was one man prepared to disregard gossip and slander – a man prepared to disregard everything but the one urgent and fundamental reason for the Queen's marriage. Thomas Radcliffe, Earl of Sussex, like most of his contemporaries, detested Robert Dudley, but he wrote to Secretary of State William Cecil in the month following Amye Dudley's death: 'I wish not her Majesty to linger this matter of so great importance but to choose speedily; and therein to follow so much her own affection as by the looking upon him whom she should choose, her whole being may be moved by desire; which shall be the readiest way, with the help of God, to bring us a blessed Prince.' If the Queen really loved and desired Robert Dudley, then Sussex, for his part, would be ready to sink his prejudices and love, honour and serve his enemy to the end. But the Earl found no supporters in this humane and generous attitude. Not even for the sake of a blessed prince would the nation stomach a wife-murderer, the upstart son of a notorious traitor, as their king, and pretty well everyone with an opinion on the subject agreed with Nicholas Throckmorton that the result of a Tudor–Dudley marriage would be 'the Queen our Sovereign discredited, condemned and neglected; our country ruined, undone and made prey'.

Robert was publicly exonerated by a coroner's jury, which

returned a verdict of misadventure on the unhappy Amye, and he returned to his usual place at the Queen's side. But she did not marry him. Although he was to remain her constant companion until his death twenty-eight years later, Elizabeth always insisted that they were 'just good friends', and no evidence to the contrary has ever been produced. Most probably she was speaking the literal truth. In Robert Dudley she had a good-looking, amusing, sophisticated escort, an old friend who already shared memories with her, an ideal crony now to share her leisure moments. He was, moreover, no mere lapdog but a man of initiative, able and talented, who could hold his own in any company. Yet he was still her creation, dependent in the last resort on her favour. Robert may well have been the only man Elizabeth ever loved, perhaps the only man she ever did seriously consider marrying; but, apart from the obvious political imprudence of such a step, in the end it always came back to one thing, to the basic principle which governed Elizabeth's life: 'I will have here but one mistress and no master.'

As time passed, the English people gradually became accustomed to the novel idea of a virgin Queen – of a Queen married to her kingdom and belonging to it alone – and most people found they preferred it that way, or would have done if only it had not been for a perpetual nagging worry about the future. No one who thought about the matter at all could fail to be aware that everything they most valued, their newly-established Protestant church, their freedom from foreign interference, the country's growing prosperity and prestige, all depended quite literally on the fragile thread of one woman's life. Fortunately for everyone's peace of mind, Elizabeth normally enjoyed excellent health but not even she was immune from the accidents of fate. At Hampton Court in the autumn of 1562 she succumbed to a virulent strain of smallpox and very nearly died. Not surprisingly the result was a renewed onslaught by a badly frightened Parliament beseeching the Queen to marry, or at least to name her successor.

Out of the dozen or so persons of royal descent who had sur-

vived into the 1560s, there were really only two with serious
claims to the position of her heir presumptive – one was Lady Katherine Grey, sister of the tragic Jane, and the other was Mary,
Queen of Scots. Katherine Grey might have commanded quite
an influential body of support – she was, after all, a staunch
Protestant and an Englishwoman born – but she had unfortunately turned out to be a common-place and foolish young
woman and had ruined herself with the Queen by making a
clandestine marriage, only discovered when her pregnancy
could no longer be concealed. Elizabeth had never thought
much of Lady Katherine, and now, King Henry's Will regard-
less, it was clear that her chances of recognition were nil.

Margaret Douglas, child of Queen Margaret Tudor's marriage to the Earl of Angus, who had married into a collateral
branch of the Stuart family and borne two sons – Henry, Lord
Darnley and Charles Stuart – was favoured by some English
Catholics who regarded her as 'devout and sensible'. According
to the Spanish ambassador, her claims had been canvassed during that terrifying day when Elizabeth was thought to be dying
of smallpox. But Margaret, an indefatigably ambitious mama,
who was twice to incur the Queen's severe displeasure for her
match-making activities, was never really a serious contender
in the succession stakes. Her niece, the Queen of Scots, had an
undeniably superior hereditary right, and in private conversation Elizabeth was perfectly prepared to concede that she
regarded her Scottish cousin as her 'next kinswoman' and
natural heir. She would not, however, make that concession
official. She knew, none better, that the heir to the throne inevitably became a focal point for discontent, and in this case the
danger would be of a special kind. There remained in England
a minority of committed Catholics who could honestly look on
Mary Stuart not merely as the rightful heir but as the rightful
Queen, ousted by a bastard and heretical usurper. To recognize
her would, therefore, not only alarm and infuriate many loyal
Protestants but give the Catholics new hope and even perhaps
tempt some among them to hasten the processes of nature. In
any case, nothing would budge Elizabeth from her absolute

determination never to live in the shadow of her successor, never to risk being 'buried alive' as her sister had been. She was well aware of the other risk she was taking in a society where 'upon the death of princes the law dieth', but her instinct was still to do nothing, to wait and see if the problem would in time resolve itself and, in the meantime, to go on gambling on her own survival. And Elizabeth Tudor, a woman isolated in a world of men, was always ready to back her instinct and her judgement, against every masculine argument of prudence, expediency and plain common sense.

The Queen's refusal to behave like a sensible man, to come to firm, logical decisions and stick to them, not infrequently drove her sensible male councillors to near despair. 'God send our mistress a husband and by time a son, that we may hope our posterity shall have a masculine succession,' wrote William Cecil on one such occasion. But Elizabeth was not to be deflected from her maddeningly devious, capricious and apparently wilful feminine ways; from her habit of leaving the logical decisions (and the logical mistakes) to others; from her guiding principle of flexibility, of always leaving her options open and never, never allowing herself to be manoeuvred into a corner by anyone. The Queen knew what she was doing – even if, quite often, no one else did – and would play the game of statecraft by her own rules or not at all.

The problem of the succession would not, of course, go away, and the closely-related problem of the Queen of Scots was soon to become acute. Mary, widowed at eighteen by the death of her French husband, had returned to her northern kingdom in the autumn of 1561. Six years and two disastrous marriages later, she landed on the coast of Cumberland, a fugitive with nothing but the clothes she stood up in, and the stage was set for another life and death struggle between two women – between the Protestant Queen and her *de facto* Catholic heiress. Mary, that romantic and calamity-prone heroine, was to prove a dangerous and determined enemy. During the long years she spent under restraint in England, she worked out her frustrations and her nervous energy in an apparently unceasing series of intrigues to gain her freedom and her cousin's throne, but, typically enough, Elizabeth consistently refused to take the obvious and logical course of action – action consistently urged upon her by her anxious well-wishers – to cut off the Scottish Queen's head and make no more ado about her. In this case, though, the pressure became, in the end, irresistible. Increasingly threatened by Catholic aggression from without and by fears of Catholic renascence from within, a point was reached when the Protestant state could quite simply no longer contain the Catholic heir. Mary's execution was perhaps the one occasion when Council and Parliament together, backed by a weight of public opinion united as never before, did finally succeed in manœuvring their slippery sovereign lady into a corner – a fact which probably accounts for some at least of her frantic, hysterical reaction after the deed was done.

But not even Elizabeth could deny that her life was easier without the ever-present shadow cast by the Queen of Scots. For one thing, the problem of the succession had at last resolved itself. In Mary Stuart's Protestant son, a king doubly descended from Henry VII, was the obvious heir, acceptable to everybody but the irreconcilable Catholic fringe and, by all accounts, a likely youth who would be ready to take over when the time came. But the time was not yet. In the 1580s Elizabeth was still very much alive and in command. After the ignominious failure of the long-heralded, much-dreaded Spanish invasion, her own and the country's international prestige had rocketed. To her fellow monarchs the Queen of England was a prodigy, a veritable *stupor mindi* – 'only a woman, only mistress of half an island, and yet she makes herself feared by Spain, by France, by all'. To her subjects she had become a cult figure, the embodiment of every goddess of classical mythology they'd ever heard of; every heroine from their favourite reading, the Bible. She was Judith and Deborah, Diana the Huntress and the Queen of the Amazons, all rolled into one. She was Gloriana and Oriana and a surrogate Virgin Mary, while still remaining their own loved and familiar Queen – especially to the Londoners who naturally saw most of her in her various journeyings about the city and to and fro between the palaces of Whitehall, Greenwich and Richmond.

One young Londoner, living in the Strand near St Clement's Church, would always remember vividly how, at about five o'clock one dark December evening in the Armada year, he and his friends heard that the Queen had just gone to a Council meeting at Somerset House and were told, 'If you will see the Queen, you must come quickly.'

Then we all ran [he wrote] when the court gates were set open, and no man hindered us from coming in. There we stayed an hour and a half and the yard was full, there being a great number of torches, when the Queen came out in great state. Then we cried, 'God save your Majesty.' And the Queen turned to us and said, 'God bless you all, my good people.' Then we cried again, 'God save your Majesty.' And the Queen said again to us, 'Ye may well have a greater prince, but ye shall never have a more loving prince.' And so the Queen and the crowd there, looking upon one another a while, her Majesty departed. This wrought such an impression upon us, for shows and pageants are best seen by torch-light, that all the way long we did nothing but talk of what an admirable Queen she was, and how we would all adventure our lives in her service.

In 1593 Elizabeth celebrated her sixtieth birthday, a considerable age for those times, but the Queen, who had already lived longer than any member of the Tudor family, was still amazingly fit and active, still dancing, riding and hunting tirelessly. André de Maisse, a French diplomat who came to England on a special mission in 1597, commented on the liveliness she displayed, both in body and mind, and apart from her face, which looked 'very aged', and her teeth, which were bad, he thought it would not be possible to find a woman 'of so fine and vigorous disposition'.

To outsiders the Queen was invariably charming, gracious and dignified; in the relative privacy of the household she could be exacting, difficult and sometimes downright impossible. Nor can it be said that her temper showed any signs of mellowing with age. She continued to rap out her 'wonted oaths' and was not above throwing things when in a tantrum, or boxing the ears of any unfortunate maid of honour who happened to annoy her. But her bark was usually worse than her bite, and when she smiled, wrote her godson John Harington, 'it was a pure sunshine that all could bask in'. Her charm and her fascination remained irresistible. As Christopher Hatton put it, 'the Queen did fish for men's souls, and had so sweet a bait that no one could escape her network'.

Elizabeth's last years brought little respite from her public burden. War with Spain and the troubles in Ireland were draining her carefully-hoarded reserves of cash at a frightening rate, and there was increasing faction within the Court between the young Turks, led by the Earl of Essex, and the more conservative element which followed sober Robert Cecil. Like many ageing people, the Queen suffered the recurrent grief of seeing old friends dying off and had to face problems of adjustment to a new generation which she did not always understand and found unsympathetic to work with. She stayed in harness to the end, but when death came for her in her seventieth year she scarcely bothered to put up a fight. She had ruled her people for nearly forty-five years, and she was handing over a nation strong, prosperous and united. The royal prerogative she had guarded so jealously was still intact, and the prestige of the monarchy had never been higher. Her task was done, and it seemed she was content to go.

England has never had another leader even remotely comparable to Elizabeth Tudor. She remains unique, the ultimate secret of her genius still unpenetrated, though perhaps Robert Cecil came nearest to it when he remarked that the Queen 'was more than a man and, in troth, sometimes less than a woman'.

Elizabethan
Women

It might be supposed that in a country governed by a spectacu-
larly successful unmarried Queen, the status of women generally and of unmarried women in particular would have
improved, but this does not seem to have been the case. No
doubt there were other women who shared the Queen's
peculiar aversion to matrimony, but the Queen was uniquely
fortunate in being free to indulge her whim to stay single,
and, in a society which continued to regard wife- and mother-
hood as woman's natural destiny, the ordinary spinster's
lot continued to be an unhappy one. Branded as a failure or
a freak or both, she could normally expect little more than a
life of dependent drudgery under some charitable relation's
roof.

As a career woman, the Queen was also unique, and yet for
the resolute minority – whether married or single – who found
themselves faced with the necessity of earning a living, opportunities, though limited, were by no means non-existent. Apart
from domestic service – often a stepping-stone to marriage –
wet and dry nursing, governessing or a position as 'waiting
gentlewoman' in a great household, the commonest female
occupations were tailoring, upholstery, millinery, embroidery
and related trades. But innkeeping was also considered acceptable, and there were plenty of laundresses, fishwives and other
street vendors, as well as a few wax-chandlers, brewers, bakers
and confectioners, even some female ironmongers and shoe-
makers. Some enterprising women set up in business as herbal-
ists, concocting cosmetics and perfumed washes, and, of more

dubious respectability, there were astrologers, fortune-tellers and quack medical practitioners. Probably the most sought-after and popular career was that of midwife, for 'Many a good thing passes through the Midwife's hand, many a merry tale by her mouth, many a glad cup through her lips. She is a leader of wives, the lady of light hearts and the queen of Gossips.' Certain trade guilds were open to women, and marriage to a member of a guild conferred rights on a wife which she retained in widowhood and could pass on to a second husband – a privilege which made such ladies especially eligible. Although the professions remained closed, women were making undeniable progress in the business world, and their value as partners and helpmeets was becoming increasingly recognized by sensible, forward-looking husbands.

Nevertheless, for the vast majority of women, housewifery was still the career for which they prepared and which they looked forward to, and in an age when self-sufficiency was no fad but a stern, practical necessity, the proper care and management of a household offered a highly-skilled, challenging and responsible occupation. The average housewife was expected to brew the family's beer and bake its bread as a matter of course, to spin, weave and make up the wool and linen cloth for clothes and household use. She must know all the techniques for preserving food – how to cure bacon and hams, to salt the meat from the autumn slaughtering which must last through the winter, store apples and vegetables for the long months when no fresh produce would be available, make jellies, conserves and pickles to vary a monotonous diet and help to conceal the taste of anything that was going 'off'. The housewife who failed to plan her winter stores adequately would know the ultimate shame of seeing her family go hungry. In most households the rush or wax lights which provided the only illumination were made at home, and so was soap – a laborious process involving mutton fat and lye, obtained from wood ash. Wash-day itself was hard labour, steeping and then beating the heavy linen sheets with wooden bats, before bleaching, smoothing and folding. Not surprisingly, this immense effort was undertaken only every three months or so. The dairy was always a good housewife's special responsibility, and she had to know enough about animal husbandry to be a judge of a milch cow. She did her own milking, reared the calves, made her own butter and cheese. She looked after the poultry, carefully hoarding feathers for pillows and mattresses, grew her own vegetables, herbs and flowers, and all this on top of the daily chores of cooking, scrubbing, sweeping and caring for her children.

Any housewife worthy of the name would have a general knowledge of sick-nursing and rudimentary doctoring, and this in turn often meant a wide knowledge of the medicinal properties of plants and herbs. In many families recipes for salves, cordials, poultices, possets and other sovereign remedies were handed down from mother to daughter, and some women with a special gift or interest in the subject would experiment on their own account. The really dedicated housewife also found time to embroider her linen and bed-hangings, distil perfume, make wines and syrups, potpourri and pastilles to be burned in a sickroom or to sweeten the air.

The larger the household, the greater the housewife's responsibilities. She had to watch over the physical and moral welfare of her maids, keep them from idleness, teach them their duties and often arrange their marriages and provide a dowry, in addition to instructing her own daughters and the daughters of friends entrusted to her care. No matter how large her staff, she still supervised all the main departments, the kitchen, pantry, buttery, stillroom, laundry and dairy, to ensure that the servants were doing their work and that waste and pilferage were kept to a minimum. She would doctor the family and household and often the surrounding neighbourhood as well. She would see to it that the 'broken meats' went down to the porter's lodge for the poor, always be prepared to offer hospitality to passing travellers or chance guests, and remember her Christian duty to care for the needs of her husband's tenants and poorer neighbours. She would be responsible for ordering supplies of anything which could not be made or grown on the estate, not unlike the quartermaster of a small army – and in her husband's absence or incapacity would cheerfully take on the management of the estate itself.

Few great ladies shirked their domestic responsibilities. Margaret Hoby, a wealthy and beautiful woman, conscientiously superintended the dyeing and winding of yarn, the making of wax candles, sweetmeats, preserves and perfumes, and would sit spinning with her maids or working at her embroidery while a devotional book was read aloud. Even the formidable Bess of Hardwick took an acute and detailed interest in the running of her numerous establishments. After the Queen, Bess was probably the richest and most influential woman in England, but unlike the Queen her career had been founded on marriage. From comparatively humble beginnings she had climbed, via a succession of fortunately-chosen husbands, to become Countess of Shrewsbury, an enormously successful business woman and inspired builder of houses. Hardwick Hall, proud, elegant and graceful on its Derbyshire ridge and the only one of her creations to survive, was built to her specifications, and she personally watched over the progress of the work, keeping a sharp eye on the accounts and tolerating no slackness or scamping.

As well as being a property tycoon, financier, farmer and dealer in lead, coal and timber, Lady Shrewsbury found plenty of time for more feminine pursuits and, like many of her contemporaries, was a skilled and enthusiastic needlewoman. The huge tapestries, usually depicting some biblical or classical theme, which covered the walls in most great houses and kept out some of the draughts, were woven in professional workrooms, but quantities of bed-curtains, counterpanes, hangings and cushions were required and needlework 'carpets' covered every available surface in houses like Hardwick. These, and the fashion for decorating caps, gloves, purses, baby clothes, shifts, smocks, men's shirts – everything, in fact, that was capable of being embroidered – offered plenty of scope for all those thousands of busy ladies and gentlewoman who 'wrought needlework'. Some ladies, such as the Queen of Scots who was a notable exponent of the art, employed a professional embroiderer to draw patterns and fill in the boring bits of background, but the artistically inclined would create their own designs and the quality of English work was deservedly famous.

William Harrison in his *Description of England* commended the older ladies of the Elizabethan Court for their industry in needlework, caulwork (a kind of ornamental netting) and spinning of silk. Others, it seemed, in their anxiety to 'shun and avoid idleness' spent their free time in 'continual reading either of the Holy Scriptures or histories of our own or foreign nations about us, and divers in writing volumes of their own, or translating of other men's into our English and Latin tongue'. Meanwhile, 'the youngest sort' applied themselves to their lutes, citterns, prick song and all kinds of music for their recreation.

Many young girls were now spending more and more of their lesson time on music, dancing and needlework and less on formal study, for as the century progressed the Renaissance dream was fading and ladies able to converse learnedly in Latin and Greek became fewer. Harrison speaks of the 'many gentlewomen and ladies there are that beside sound knowledge of the Greek and Latin tongues, are thereto no less skilful in the Spanish, Italian and French', but in general these were of the older generation – women like Mildred Burghley and Anne Bacon – and by the end of the Elizabethan period it was becoming fashionable to poke fun at female learning. This decline was partly due to the fact that there was no royal schoolroom to give a lead, no young princesses to be imitated and the Court, although it remained a brilliant social and political centre, was no longer a centre of higher thought. Nor was it ever in any sense a centre of feminism. The Queen had some women friends, the Marchioness of Northampton, Lady Norris and the Countess of Nottingham among them, but she did not welcome competition from her own sex and at Court it was the men who counted. The ladies of the household, never very many in number, were not encouraged to put themselves forward and Elizabeth, perhaps regrettably, showed no interest whatever in the liberation of women.

All the same, progress had been made. The Elizabethan woman certainly did not regard herself as a chattel and most middle- and upper-class girls now learnt to read and write as a matter of course, while some of the old rigid notions about the unquestioning obedience of daughters had begun to show signs of relaxation. In any case, the Queen's female subjects were not complaining. They painted their faces, curled, dyed and pomaded their hair, played cards, danced, were seen at the theatre and generally took a lively part in the social round untroubled by doubts or discontents about their place in society. The quality of life for both men and women had unquestionably improved during the Tudor century, and that was enough for most people.

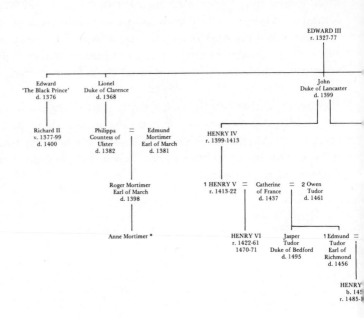

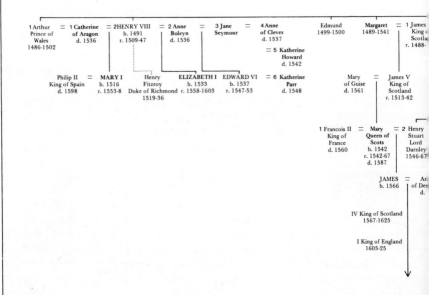

EDWARD III
r. 1327-77

Edward
'The Black Prince'
d. 1376

Lionel
Duke of Clarence
d. 1368

John
Duke of Lancaster
d. 1399

Richard II
v. 1377-99
d. 1400

Philippa
Countess of
Ulster
d. 1382

= Edmund
Mortimer
Earl of March
d. 1381

HENRY IV
r. 1399-1413

Roger Mortimer
Earl of March
d. 1398

1 HENRY V
r. 1413-22

= Catherine
of France
d. 1437

= 2 Owen
Tudor
d. 1461

Anne Mortimer *

HENRY VI
r. 1422-61
1470-71

Jasper
Tudor
Duke of Bedford
d. 1495

1 Edmund =
Tudor
Earl of
Richmond
d. 1456

HENRY
b. 145
r. 1485-

1 Arthur
Prince of
Wales
1486-1502

= 1 Catherine
of Aragon
d. 1536

= 2 HENRY VIII
b. 1491
r. 1509-47

= 2 Anne
Boleyn
d. 1536

= 3 Jane
Seymour

= 4 Anne
of Cleves
d. 1537

= 5 Katherine
Howard
d. 1542

Edmund
1499-1500

Margaret
1489-1541

= 1 James
King o
Scotla
r. 1488-

Philip II
King of Spain
d. 1598

= MARY I
b. 1516
r. 1553-8

Henry
Fitzroy
Duke of Richmond
1519-36

ELIZABETH I
b. 1533
r. 1558-1603

EDWARD VI
b. 1537
r. 1547-53

= 6 Katherine
Parr
d. 1548

Mary
of Guise
d. 1561

= James V
King of
Scotland
r. 1513-42

1 Francois II
King of
France
d. 1560

= Mary
Queen of
Scots
b. 1542
r. 1542-67
d. 1587

= 2 Henry
Stuart
Lord
Darnley
1546-67

JAMES
b. 1566

= Ar
of Des
d.

IV King of Scotland
1567-1625

I King of England
1603-25

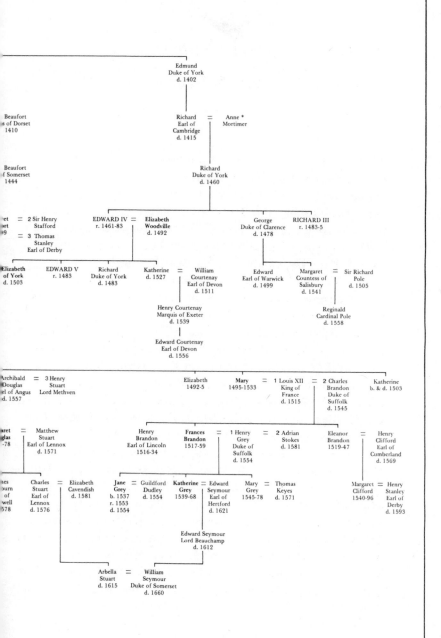

Edmund
Duke of York
d. 1402

Beaufort
s of Dorset
1410

Richard = Anne *
Earl of   Mortimer
Cambridge
d. 1415

Beaufort
f Somerset
1444

Richard
Duke of York
d. 1460

ret = 2 Sir Henry   EDWARD IV = Elizabeth   George   RICHARD III
rt   Stafford   r. 1461-83   Woodville   Duke of Clarence r. 1483-5
9   = 3 Thomas   d. 1492   d. 1478
       Stanley
       Earl of Derby

Elizabeth   EDWARD V   Richard   Katherine = William   Edward   Margaret   = Sir Richard
of York   r. 1483   Duke of York d. 1527   Courtenay   Earl of Warwick Countess of   Pole
d. 1503   d. 1483   Earl of Devon   d. 1499   Salisbury   d. 1505
                                                 d. 1511   d. 1541

                                     Henry Courtenay   Reginald
                                     Marquis of Exeter   Cardinal Pole
                                     d. 1539   d. 1558

                                     Edward Courtenay
                                     Earl of Devon
                                     d. 1556

rchibald = 3 Henry   Elizabeth   Mary   = 1 Louis XII = 2 Charles   Katherine
Douglas   Stuart   1492-5   1495-1533   King of   Brandon   b. & d. 1503
rl of Angus Lord Methven   France   Duke of
d. 1557   d. 1515   Suffolk
                                                                                    d. 1545

ret = Matthew   Henry   Frances = 1 Henry   = 2 Adrian   Eleanor   = Henry
glas   Stuart   Brandon   Brandon   Grey   Stokes   Brandon   Clifford
-78   Earl of Lennox   Earl of Lincoln 1517-59 Duke of   d. 1581   1519-47   Earl of
       d. 1571   1516-34   Suffolk   Cumberland
                                                     d. 1554   d. 1569

es   Charles = Elizabeth   Jane = Guildford Katherine = Edward   Mary   = Thomas   Margaret = Henry
urn   Stuart   Cavendish   Grey   Dudley   Grey   Seymour   Grey   Keyes   Clifford   Stanley
of   Earl of   d. 1581   b. 1537 d. 1554   1539-68   Earl of   1545-78 d. 1571   1540-96   Earl of
well   Lennox   r. 1553   Hertford   Derby
78   d. 1576   d. 1554   d. 1621   d. 1593

                                                 Edward Seymour
                                                 Lord Beauchamp
                                                 d. 1612

                      Arbella = William
                      Stuart   Seymour
                      d. 1615   Duke of Somerset
                                 d. 1660

A Note
on Sources

There's an enormous mass of published material on virtually every aspect of the Tudor century and for anyone wanting to embark on a detailed study, the OUP *Bibliography of British History – Tudor Period*, edited by Conyers Read, 1959, is an essential tool. Another, more portable but still very useful bibliography is *Tudor England*, edited by Mortimer Levine and published by the CUP for the Conference on British Studies in 1968.

The list which follows is obviously brief and is intended as no more than a guide to those printed sources and secondary works which I have found most helpful.

Two good general surveys are *The Elizabethan Woman: A Panorama of English Womanhood, 1540–1640* by Carroll Camden, 1952, and *Elizabethans at Home*, Lu E. Pearson, Stanford, 1957, both of which contain good bibliographies. *A Relation ... of the Island of England*, C. A. Sneyd, Camden Society, old series, xxxvii, 1847, and *England as Seen by Foreigners*, W. B. Rye, 1865, are interesting for an outside view of the English scene. For the educational revolution see *Vives and the Renascence Education of Women*, ed. Foster Watson, 1912. Vols IV and V of John Leland's *De Rebus Britannicis Collectanea* (not all in Latin, despite its title) ed. Thomas Hearne, Oxford, 1715, give details of Lady Margaret Beaufort's ordinances and also a description of Margaret Tudor's betrothal. For a life of Lady Margaret herself, see *Lady Margaret, Mother of Henry VII*, E. M. G. Routh, 1925, and for her daughter-in-law *The Privy Purse Expenses of Elizabeth of York with a Memoir*, N. H. Nicolas, 1830 (reissued in a limited facsimile edition in 1972).

There are antiquated but still perfectly useful biographies of the Princesses Margaret and Mary in *The Lives of the Princesses of England*, M. A. E. Green, 6 vols, 1849–55. A modern account is *The Sisters of Henry VIII*, Hester Chapman 1969.

Most of Henry VIII's wives have attracted the attention of biographers and *Catherine of Aragon*, Garrett Mattingly, 1942, is an outstanding example of everything a biography should be. Paul Friedmann's *Anne Boleyn – A Chapter of English History*, 2 vols, 1884, is still the classic work on Anne, but there have been two recent lives, *Anne Boleyn* by Marie Louise Bruce, 1972, and *Anne Boleyn*, Hester Chapman, 1974. There are no full-length modern lives of Jane Seymour or Anne of Cleves, but there's a section on Jane in *Ordeal by Ambition*, a general account of the Seymour family under the Tudors by William Seymour, 1972. For Katherine Howard see *A Tudor Tragedy*, Lacey Baldwin Smith, 1961, and for Katherine Parr, *Queen Katherine Parr*, Anthony Martienssen, 1973. There are biographies of all the queens in Agnes Strickland's *Lives of the Queens of England*, 8 vols, 1851. These are old-fashioned and not always entirely reliable but still well worth reading.

The Chronicle of Queen Jane, J. G. Nichols, Camden Society, xlviii, 1850, is a marvellous contemporary source and also contains a description of Mary's wedding to Philip of Spain. There are lives of Jane and her sisters in *The Lives of the Tudor Princesses*, Agnes Strickland, 1868. For a modern biography of Jane, see *Lady Jane Grey*, Hester Chapman, 1962, and for Katherine Grey, *Two Tudor Portraits*, Hester Chapman, 1960.

The most illuminating source material for Mary's life and reign are the despatches of Eustace Chapuys and Simon Renard in the Calendar of State Papers, Spanish, 13 vols, 1862–1954. Of the handful of modern lives, *Mary Tudor* by H. F. M. Prescott, revised edition, 1952, is first-rate and contains a helpful note on sources as well as a full bibliography.

Much of the material on the first twenty-five years of Elizabeth's life is printed in handy form in *The Girlhood of Queen Elizabeth*, F. A. Mumby, 1909. *Queen Elizabeth I*, J. E. Neale's classic biography first published in 1934 and reprinted many times since, remains the best modern life, but *Elizabeth I: A study in power and intellect*, Paul Johnson, 1974, is excellent on the political side and *Elizabeth the Great* by Elizabeth Jenkins, 1958, probably the best of the more 'personal' accounts. For modern studies of the Queen's relationship with Robert Dudley, see *Elizabeth and Leicester*, Milton Waldman, 1944, and *Elizabeth and Leicester*, Elizabeth Jenkins, 1961. Other sources which give personal glimpses of the Queen are, among many, *The Progresses ... of Queen Elizabeth*, J. Nichols, 3 vols, 1823; *Nugae Antiquae* by John Harington, ed. Thomas Park, 1804, and André de Maisse's *Journal*, trans. G. B. Harrison, 1931.

A Tudor Tapestry, Derek Wilson, 1972, gives an interesting account of Anne Askew and *My Lady of Suffolk: A Portrait of Catherine Willoughby*, E. Read, New York, 1963, and the *Diary of Lady Margaret Hoby*, D. M. Meads, 1930, are both valuable for insights into religious life.

Index

Elizabeth I – *continued*
158; the succession question,
159, 160; execution of Mary
Stuart, 161; death (1603), 163;
other references, 71, 83, 105,
106, 115, 125, 127, 131, 147,
149, 150–3, 164, 167–9
Elizabeth, Princess (daughter of
Henry VII), 17, 20
Elizabeth of York (consort of
Henry VII), 5, 12, 14–21, 23–5
English Prayer Book (1552), 125
Erasmus, Desiderius, 2, 34
Essex, Earl of, 163
Eton College, 107
Exeter, Marchioness of, 85

Ferdinand, King of Aragon, 28, 29
de Feria, Count, 3, 153
Ferretti, Francesco, 3
Fisher, John (Bishop of Rochester),
8, 14, 22, 26, 27, 71
Fitzwilliam, Lady, 108
Flodden, Battle of (1513), 31
Fotheringay, 115
Foxe, John, 109
Framlingham Castle, 133
France, 16, 39, 87, 115
François I, King of France, 42, 86
François II, King of France,
160, *see also* Dauphin, the
de Fresnada, Francisco, 152

Gardiner, Stephen (Bishop of
Winchester), 59, 109, 110, 111,
112
Gaunt, John of (Duke of
Lancaster), 7
Germany, 87, 150
Gigs, Margaret, 34
Gomez, Ruy, 144
Greenwich Palace, 30, 33, 69, 78,
106, 162
Grey, Frances (née Brandon),
Marchioness of Dorset, Duchess
of Suffolk, 114, 121, 124, 128
Grey, Henry (Marquess of Dorset,

Duke of Suffolk), 114, 119, 121,
122, 134, 140
Grey, Lady Jane, 114, 116, 119,
121, 122, 127–9, 131, 132, 134,
140–2, 159
Grey, Katherine, 114, 159
Grey, Mary, 114
Grindal, William, 106
Grocyn, William, 34
Guise, Mary of (Queen Dowager
and Regent of Scotland), 115

Hall, Edward, 54, 55
Hampton Court Palace, 78, 84,
100, 103, 107, 147–9, 158
Hanworth, Middlesex, 120
Hardwick Hall, 167
Harington, Sir John, 163
Harrison, William, 168
Hastings, Sir Edward, 133
Hatfield, Hertfordshire, 122, 123,
150, 153
Hatton, Christopher, 163
Hayward, John, 155
Henri II, King of France, 115
Henry VI, King of England, 7, 10
Henry VII, King of England, 8, 10,
13–16, 20, 21, 23, 25, 26, 29, 114
Henry VIII, King of England: birth
(1491), 17; marriage to
Catherine of Aragon (1509), 28,
30–3; pursuit of Anne Boleyn,
46, 47; start of annulment of
marriage to Catherine of
Aragon, 49–51; 'the King's
Great Matter', 52–4; Act of
Supremacy, 59; creates Anne
Boleyn Marquess of Pembroke,
59; marriage with Anne Boleyn
(1533), 60–2; annulment of
marriage with Catherine of
Aragon, 66; coronation of Anne
Boleyn, 66; 1st Act of Succession
(1534), 69; execution of Thomas
More and John Fisher, 70, 71;
death of Catherine of Aragon,
72; wooing of Jane Seymour, 72;
arrest of Anne Boleyn, 74;

INDEX